Starting a Successful Psychology and Counseling

Clinical and counseling psychology are rapidly growing yet challenging professions: the preparation is arduous, the training is highly selective, and the results—an established and financially successful practice—are not easy to achieve. This book explains how to prepare for and surmount all of the hurdles presented to those who hope to eventually develop a lucrative and rewarding practice in clinical psychology. It is the first of its kind to focus primarily on financial success, though it does also look at the personal stresses and rewards of the profession. The author provides tips from his own experience and from other financially successful private practice psychologists, and offers business techniques and pointers that are not explained in training programs. Undergraduate students contemplating a career in psychology will find advice on preparing for the GRE (Graduate Record Examination), applying to graduate schools, and getting involved in research and clinical work. For graduate students, an overview of a graduate clinical psychology program, preparing and completing a dissertation, and gaining experience in psychological testing are provided. Chapters then focus on how to build and manage a private practice, the best ways to manage personal and business finances, and how to practice good self-care. Additionally, the book includes a chapter by an expert on student-loan repayment that examines how to best work through the process of paying back student loans while building a practice.

Owen J. Bargreen, PsyD, is a Seattle-area private practice psychologist who specializes in school violence, domestic violence, and personality and cognitive assessment. He is an affiliate professor of psychology at Trinity Lutheran College in Everett, WA.

Starting a Successful Practice in Clinical Psychology and Counseling

A Guide for Students in Psychology and New Career Psychologists

Owen J. Bargreen

Routledge
Taylor & Francis Group

NEW YORK AND LONDON

First published 2014
by Routledge
711 Third Avenue, New York, NY 10017

Simultaneously published in the UK
by Routledge
27 Church Road, Hove, East Sussex BN3 2FA

*Routledge is an imprint of the Taylor & Francis Group,
an informa business*

© 2014 Taylor & Francis

Library of Congress Cataloging-in-Publication Data
Bargreen, Owen J.
 Starting a successful practice in clinical psychology and counseling : a guide
for students in psychology and new career psychologists / Owen J. Bargreen.
  pages cm
  Includes index.
1. Clinical psychology—Practice.   2. Psychotherapy—Practice.
3. Counselors—Training of.   4. Psychotherapists—Training of.   I. Title.
  RC467.B355 2013
  616.890068—dc23
  2013014390

ISBN: 978-0-415-83294-6 (hbk)
ISBN: 978-0-415-83295-3 (pbk)
ISBN: 978-0-203-50794-0 (ebk)

Typeset in Caslon
by Apex CoVantage, LLC

SFI Certified Sourcing
www.sfiprogram.org
SFI-00453

Printed and bound in the United States of America
by Edwards Brothers, Inc.

Contents

Acknowledgments

I couldn't have written this book without the fantastic support of my parents, Howie and Melinda Bargreen, and my sister, Maren Bargreen Mullin. They have helped me in so many ways to become the successful man and businessman that I am today. I am eternally grateful to my grandfather, Howard Bargreen, and my grandmother, Grace Bargreen, for providing me the incredible opportunity to attend Whitman College, where I found a good deal of my original interest and influence in the field of psychology. I would like to thank my inspirational graduate school professors and supervisors, particularly Dr. Martin Landau-North, Dr. Michael Wrobel, Dr. James Madero, Dr. Jose Lichtszajn, and Dr. Jon Nachison, for their help in guiding me through the daunting task of getting through graduate school. Finally, I would like to thank my friends, particularly Ross Field, Tim Mullin, and psychologists Dr. Ian Wolds, Dr. Danny Tucker, Dr. Will Zahn, Dr. Renee Low, and Dr. JD Friedman, for their support over the years. People tell me that I have great friends and I feel that I have the best friends of anyone I know.

1

How Can I Help You Make Money?

Why Write This Book?

Many people ask me why I should write a book that helps other psychologists make more money. That is a very complex question. The answer is multi-faceted. I want to help you. When you do better, the profession does better. Ultimately, it is about the advancement of the profession. The more that you make, the more others will make. We all want to earn money, but we want to feel good doing so. With the proper foundation, you can be financially successful and feel good about helping others. There is some natural cognitive dissonance that comes with making money in psychology. I can remember the first person who paid me for therapy. I felt badly about it and my initial thoughts were that I shouldn't be receiving a good deal of money for a therapy session. An automatic thought I had was "Maybe I should be charging less." My ensuing epiphany was "I am running a business and I have innumerable expenses including student loans, mortgages, car payments, and business expenses—really too many expenses to name." My book explains that it is OK to be financially successful in our profession. You can help kids, adolescents, adults, families, and couples and feel good about getting paid to make a difference in the world. It feels good to be paid to make a difference. Really, there is no good reason not to be financially successful. There are some sacrifices that you will need to make, but it will be worth it. By making good money, you will be protecting your future. I promise to explain more about that later.

Psychologists face some grave issues. Reimbursement rates for psychologists are declining. When the Medicare reimbursement goes down for psychologists, so too do the other insurance reimbursements. Then, sooner or later, the private pay reimbursements go down (this is not an acceptable trend). After what we have been through in grad school, and licensing, I am all for psychologists making money. When you make more money, I make more money. That is not a bad deal for me. I was able to be successful in a short period of time and I want you to be successful as well. Grad school was a long, arduous experience, and at times it can seem like a complete nightmare: the coursework, the dissertation, dealing with the administration. It can also be a wonderful time to blossom, because there are many meaningful clinical and research learning opportunities.

I do a substantial amount of psychological testing. With the poor reimbursement rates for psychologists out there, I am careful about what I choose to do. And I am sometimes asked why I do not do psychological testing for a cheap reimbursement rate. The reason is simple . . . doing our work for cheap is not good for the future of the profession. There is a great difference between doing pro-bono work and doing work for a rate more than 20 percent below the standard charge for testing services, which in my state in 2013 is less than $100 an hour. The former is encouraged and should be a part of everyone's private practice, while the latter is not acceptable. When I do not do the work for substandard rates, I am doing a big favor the rest of the profession. The more work that we do cheaply, the more that people will look down on our profession. And we are already getting plenty of that from other professions, particularly the medical field. It is important for us to stand up for our profession. Whether that means getting involved with your state psychological association or joining APA, we need to do our best to protect the integrity of what we do. Psychology has been challenged for many years and we face tough times, as social programs are getting cut, reimbursement rates have decreased, and master's level therapists are everywhere. This can create the impression that psychologists aren't as valuable as they, in fact, truly are. Psychologists are not making money that is consistent with their experience and education. But, there is a method to making more money as a psychologist.

We are taught not to look out for ourselves. Psychologists abide by possibly the toughest ethical code of conduct compared to other professions. We are so worried about being sued, doing the wrong thing, and saying something that we shouldn't, that we don't do a better job protecting our rights. Many psychologists are practicing in fear, which sometimes prevents them from making more money. Now I am not saying that everyone should do high-risk work like child-custody evaluations. We need, however, to look out for our profession more closely and not be as fearful. I certainly have been guilty of being fearful quite a few times. And the fear is not unfounded. We hear about these horrible cases where psychologists, as a result of vengeful lawsuits by divorcing spouses, lose their licenses. We go through years of laws and ethics classes so that we understand what is and what is not acceptable conduct in our profession. We are really left with little margin for error, as sometimes even the slightest error can cause major ethical problems. Any breach of confidentiality and we can be sued. We are going to make errors but it is unlikely that we are going to make ethical violations. I shouldn't have to tell you that you shouldn't solicit patients—there are better ways to make money. Besides, the APA Ethics Code directly tells us that it is not OK to solicit patients, as we cannot misuse our influence as psychologists.

Did you always know that you wanted to be a psychologist? Chances are, you didn't know that before attending undergraduate studies. Perhaps you were inspired as an undergrad, just as I was. I will explain to you what you need to do during your undergrad years in order to move forward toward the goal of becoming a clinical psychologist. Not to increase your pressure, but doing well in undergrad courses will be more important than you think, as more and more people apply for clinical psychology programs. So be sure to not blow off your grades, even if you are attending a great school, because many schools will have cutoff GPAs (grade point average) where you simply won't meet their criteria unless you are above what they are looking for. Brutal, huh?

Maybe you have already completed graduate school. Well, what do you learn in graduate school? You learn about psychology. You learn about theory, research, psychotherapy, and psychological testing. Grad school provides some essential information about the practice of psychology. As I'll explain later, grad school offers some incredible opportunities to gain experience doing psychological testing (hopefully). And of course there are great opportunities to gain skills as a therapist as well.

But what about the business side of the practice? Maybe you have a class that includes a few lectures regarding the business side of practicing psychology. That's what my program did. A few lectures weren't enough. Did you have a class on business? Maybe two classes? Not likely. I had to know more. So I did my research. Fortunately, my father was an MBA with a good deal of business experience, so he mentored me. But what about the people who don't have a dad who is in business? This book will help you from the business perspective. While I don't have my business degree, I do know how to make money and I know how to create a profitable business. Bill Gates didn't have a business degree either. And he's not exactly panhandling on the street.

I'm not going to pretend that I know everything about business. But I can offer some good advice about creating a financially successful practice in clinical psychology. That's what I did. I started my practice in Fall 2008. By Fall 2009, I was having $50K quarters. That equates to $200K each year (for those who struggle through the arithmetic section of the WAIS-IV). We are talking about a serious income here. I don't have a family but that is the kind of income that can easily support a family. And if you want three-plus kids, you will likely need a large income to support the family.

Money makes everything easier. Don't tell me that you want to come out of grad school and make $60K per year. Now I am sure that there are those who say that they really don't care about how much they make. I'm not going to believe that for a minute. Most people care, even those with a doctorate in psychology. That doesn't mean that you don't want to help people, but everyone who finishes a five- to six-year doctorate wants to make good money when they are done. They want to, because they feel that they have earned their stripes. They feel entitled to making more money than the rest. And they will make more money than others in mental health, excluding psychiatrists.

We live in a capitalistic society. So far, capitalism, compared to other economic systems, seems to be working adequately. But it is a double-edged sword. As psychologists, we have a drive to help, to work through people's problems and to enhance the lives of others. But trust me, when you start making money in your practice, you are going to want to make more and more. Darwin calls this "survival of the fittest," in that we want to do the best to ensure our survival. Making a good salary is one way of ensuring our survival. It is also a way to protect and support our offspring, another Darwinian point. I would argue that the need to create financial security is inherent in all humans, whether they have a more altruistic bent or not. Besides, as we know through recent research on altruism, most people are not "perfectly" altruistic. I think our drive to make money is OK, and I would also say that the drive to make money is essential for the future integrity of our profession. If we don't do well financially, Medicaid rates go down, insurance rates go down, and we get paid less. The reality is that the more we make, the better or more-esteemed our profession appears.

Darwin also taught us about natural selection. Natural selection is about surviving and reproducing in the best possible fashion. For now, we will apply this to economics and leave out the sex talk. If you want to have the nice things, drive the nice car, then read on. Darwin tells us that humans try to carry on the best traits or attributes to subsequent generations. He tells us that some people are going to be more successful (economically, in this case) than others. Those who are successful will continue to strive for success in order to carry those traits that will enhance the advancement of their offspring. What does this have to do with psychology? Well, if you have a financially successful practice, you will be anchoring the future of the profession. We have a natural need to try to do better, and to do better financially because that will enhance our lives, and ultimately our species and our profession. By doing better financially, we will work to maintain the survival of our species (clinical psychology). This is how humans evolve (Darwin) and how our profession evolves (psychology). Now, this is not the ultimate evolution of the practice of psychology. But we are talking about a marked improvement about the quality of life in clinicians. I would argue that when clinicians' lives are improved, the quality of their practice is likely also improved. That means better quality of service. This benefits society.

The truth is that there can be a huge discrepancy in salaries between psychologists. I mean, we are talking about someone making $50–60K and someone making $200K. That is potentially four times more money, excluding taxes. Can you imagine living in a house that was four times nicer than yours? How about driving a car that was four times nicer? Or being able to afford a house or condo at all? For those psychologists who have been in practice for many years, what about being able to pay for your kids' college tuition rather than telling them to get a job or a student loan during college? They might get a job and then drop out. They might not get a job and drop out. But I can assure you that most kids who have their college paid for are going to really appreciate what their parents are doing for them. They also will start their professional lives without a tremendous burden of debt. You are giving your kids a valuable opportunity.

For those who are younger psychologists, like myself, I don't want to burst your bubble here, but you are going to have to pay for a lot of things in your life. It is going to be hard to pay for a $200K house or condo. Eventually, you will want to buy a place and stop throwing money away with rent. With housing markets improving but banks not lending, you might have to save $100K for that, which is a hell of a lot of money. Now, unless you marry someone who is rich, or is a recipient of a fantastic trust fund, you are going to have to come up with some serious cash. It takes a very long time to come up with that kind of cash. But remember that many banks require 20 or 30 percent down for purchasing a house or condo. If you buy a house or condo that is $500K, then you will likely need at least $100K. Saving is tough. Factoring in saving with having children, and it is an even more laborious task.

Let's say that you have kids when you are 35 and you would like to save roughly $100–150K for a house or condo by the age of 55. Twenty years equals $5–7.5K per year that you will have to save, double that if you want to buy the house or condo by age 45—yep, that's saving $10–15K per year! That is a ton of money to save each year. And you will likely have to do this in order to pay for a house or condo. This task is going to be considerably easier if you are making $150K per year rather than $70K per year. Even saving for smaller things, such as a trip to Europe, is not easy. Assuming that your trip costs $5K, including airfare and hotels, it might take you an entire year to save for the trip. If you want to travel regularly, that can be a serious expense. But with the right income direction, regular travel and yearly great vacations can be a possibility. Saving is part of being financially successful, and I am going to help you work on this important issue in this book.

Making more money is about thinking about the future. It is about thinking about a better means for your family and upgrading your lifestyle. It is about paying off those student loans sooner, about having less anxiety about getting that car loan, about having (in most cases) a better quality of life. Money isn't everything, but it sure makes life easier. There has also been a trend in the past 10 to 20 years where some psychologists have been making actually less money than when they began. Some of my older psychologist colleagues complain about this all of the time—how the reimbursement rates continue to decline for insurance companies and Medicare/Medicaid. Despite increases in living and business operating costs, psychologists are actually making less money than in the mid-1990s. However, I have also found that the ones who are making less money are the ones who are only doing psychotherapy and are not doing consulting or psychological testing, which typically offer better reimbursements. Still, my colleagues' complaints highlight a disconcerting trend for the future of our profession.

While the reimbursement rates continue to decline, my book focuses on making lemonade out of lemons. We face a tough situation as psychologists today and we want to make the most out of it, financially. This book isn't only for those who have completed grad school, have fought through the EPPP (Examination for the Professional Practice of Psychology) and state licensing exams, or who have set up their private practices. This book is also for those who are considering a grad school, and for those who are still in grad school and don't know how to set up their careers. I will begin by explaining what you should do in grad school to best position yourself for money-making opportunities once you have completed licensure.

Typing

Typing is a skill that comes naturally to many. For those in my age range as a 30-something, it is very likely that you are a fast typist. I became a seasoned typist when I started my undergrad. At Whitman College, everyone was really into Instant Messaging. My girlfriend at the time was constantly on IM and messaging me. We would chat back and forth for hours, which became really silly because she was one floor down from me in the freshman dorm. Little did I know that the typing skills that I gained from constant IMing would provide a very helpful template for my current work as a psychologist. Yes, I am coming to my point here.

My point is that you need to have good keyboarding skills. If you are in grad school and are not a good typist, this is something that I feel you should address immediately. Not only will you be writing your dissertation on a computer, but you are also going to be doing a ton of work using your computer once you're in private practice. Typing on the computer is essential in psychology, especially in psychological testing. As I have stated, the best way to make money in starting a private practice is to do a lot of psychological testing. So work on your keyboarding skills if you are not a sound typist. Take a class if you need to. Get on IM and chat with friends. Just make this happen because it will be worth it in the end. My IM recommendation sounds silly, but you would be surprised how important having excellent keyboarding is in your practice. Improving your typing skills could save you hundreds of hours in your clinical practice in the future. I know that focusing on tech skills follows a problem today where the entire world has gone technological and people have lost face-to-face connections with one another. But please do this, because my book is about being financially successful. We don't live in Cuba, so you will have plenty of opportunities as a psychologist to become financially successful. If you don't make the money, someone else will. And don't tell me that you don't want that Hawaiian vacation this year.

I have colleagues who also do state assistance evaluations, as I do. They are unable to type out their evaluations immediately like I do, so it takes them substantially longer to do the psych evals. What I can get done in 45 minutes, would take some twice as long. Simple math here is that I am going to be making 100 PERCENT MORE MONEY THAN THEY DO IN A DAY DOING THE EVALUATIONS. This equates to big bucks. If I do eight evaluations in a day at $130 a pop, that equals $1,040, whereas they will be making $520. I'll take the $1,040, please.

Lately there have been major changes made to dictation software. For instance, some of my colleagues use Dragon, a new, more-seamless form of dictation software, where you can dictate into your computer and the software writes down what you say on a word processing document. This might seem easier to you, because you don't need to type things down. But remember that you will have to spend additional time with the dictation software, once you are done with your interviews and evaluations. Time is money, so it is best to learn how to type as you go during evaluations. You don't want to spend extra hours after work, whether you are typing things down or whether you are using the finest dictation software available.

Being a good typist is essential, but it is also important for you to be able to process and multitask well while typing. The art of multitasking during an evaluation requires a lot of practice. When you are typing, it is important for you to process what the person is saying. It is imperative that you gain skills that are connected to processing information quickly and being able to synthesize information cogently. Your ability to synthesize information presented to you will improve as you gain clinical experience. For instance, if you are starting graduate school, processing what the person across from you is saying will take a great deal of time. There will be a period of time in your career as a psychologist where your ability to multitask and process/synthesize information will be at its apex. Since processing speed worsens, rather than improves, with age, you also will eventually lose some abilities to process information and multitask as you grow older. Your eventual lowered ability to process information and multitask is further evidence that your most financially successful (biggest volume) years as a clinical psychologist will be when you are younger, but also will be after you have gained some clinical experience.

Making Money

You know that you didn't get into psychology to get rich, right? You should have become a medical doctor or a lawyer if you wanted to be rich. But the good news is that you have already prepared yourself well for making money by taking the psych testing classes, choosing good and varied clinical internships, etc. You did that, right? If you didn't do that, you can just take the classes over. Just kidding.

Here are the recent stats on psychologists:

Median annual wages of wage and salary clinical, counseling, and school psychologists were $76,741 in 2013 (http://www.psychology careercenter.org/salaries.html). Looking at the stats, we are not talking about a whole bunch of money. $70K, especially if you are living in a high cost-of-living space, like Southern California (So Cal) or NYC, is not going to buy you a house. If you're in So Cal, you are going to be renting a one-bedroom in Van Nuys. Rough. We are not going to think about that right now. Of course, there is a huge difference between $70K in rural environments and $70K in So Cal. There may be a 100 percent difference between the two comparisons. So you know that you want to be in the top 10 percent. And who wouldn't? $100K looks way nicer than $70K. It is also nearly 50 percent more money. Who wouldn't want to make 50 percent more money than they are currently making?

How does a psychologist's income compare with other professions? Well, the statistics are downright scary. The median pay for a psychologist is $76.7K. The median pay for a medical doctor is $166.4K. That is more than two times the pay of a psychologist. While being a medical doctor requires more years and training than for a psychologist, it is alarming that they make more than twice the salary (http://www.bls. gov/ooh/healthcare/physicians-and-surgeons.htm). Dentists, who typically do not require the same number of years to attain their doctoral degrees as do psychologists, make considerably more money than psychologists. In fact, at $146.9k per year, dentists make more than double what most psychologists make. Dental specialists, such as oral surgeons, have a median income of $217K, about three times the median income of a psychologist (http://www.bls.gov/oes/current/oes291022.htm). Does that seem fair, especially considering the amount of work required for our doctoral degrees?

Being a pharmacist does not require a doctoral degree. But the average salary of a pharmacist is $111.5K. That is almost 50 percent of what a psychologist makes. This is both brutal and disturbing (http://www.bls.gov/ooh/Healthcare/Pharmacists.htm). Even physicians assistants, who possess a Master's degree, make an average of $86.4K per year (http://www.bls.gov/ooh/healthcare/physician-assistants.htm). They are making more money than psychologists! Physical therapists, many of whom do not have a doctoral-level degree, have a median pay of $76.3k per year (http://www.bls.gov/ooh/healthcare/physical-therapists.htm). A physical therapist assistant, who has only a two-year degree, has a median pay of $51K, which is behind what most psychologists make but is on par with what some psychologists make (http://www.bls.gov/oes/current/oes312021.htm). Dental hygienists, who hold either a two-year or four-year degree, have essentially a similar median income as psychologists, $68.2K (http://www.bls.gov/ooh/healthcare/dental-hygienists.htm). That profession only requires an associate's degree! People with lower-level degrees in helping professions are making more money than psychologists. And this is a big problem.

Talking to people is an essential part of making money. You will have to learn how to sell yourself. We are taught not to sell ourselves when we are in grad school, but in the real world, you will have to sell yourself and your work, to insurance panels, school districts, hospitals, and businesses. There are certain people who are better able to talk to strangers about themselves. A more gregarious person typically is more adept at making a sale. This may be a particularly difficult process for those who are more introverted or reticent. You will have to fake it if you are not comfortable with talking about yourself. You may need to practice talking to new people with your friends or in front of a mirror.

Don't just take my opinions on making money. Read valued opinions such as Suze Orman and other famous U.S. economists. Orman has a very direct way of speaking about money. She knows business and how to save, how to make money, and what to do and what not to do financially. She has an amazing story, as she transformed her job as a housewife into becoming an economic mogul. The best economists have good advice. Also, get a financial advisor (once you've started your practice). Listen to what he/she says. This is like taking a free class in school. Free is always good. Learn about the stock market, about mutual funds, about retirement accounts such as the 401K, the ROTH

IRA, the SEP, etc. You will have to pay them for their services, but they will make you considerably more money than what you will have to pay them. Learning about the financial world and finding a good financial advisor are essential parts of becoming a better businessperson.

Setting Financial Goals

Everyone is going to have a different financial goal. For some it will be $100K per year. For others, it will be having a full practice and won't include any financial goals. I would strongly consider setting a tangible and reachable financial goal each year. Do some research and see what you need to do to reach that goal. For instance, if you want to make $100K per year, you will need to make $2K per week. Unless you work for a company where you receive paid vacation, you will have to make more than $2K per week to account for the time that you spend on vacation. If you take a whole month off, you will need to make $2.1K per week to reach that goal. What if you have the goal to make $150K per year. Lofty goal, huh? Tough, but not impossible. You are going to have to make $3K per week to achieve this. If you take a month off, you will have to make $3.2K per week.

These goals have to be attainable . . . they can't be ridiculous. For instance, average first-year psychologists are not going to make $150K. They are not likely to make $100K, either. It is going to take a few years to make $100K or more. Look, I know you are a high achiever. Perhaps you had a 4.0 GPA. all through college. But don't be ridiculous here. We didn't choose this profession to get filthy rich. We did this because we want to help people (and preferably not starve doing it). Your financial goals also have to correspond to where you are living. For instance, it is going to be easier to make $100K if you are living in NYC rather than in Topeka. But at the same time, your expenses are going to be considerably higher, so you will need to account for those factors. If you are living in a more rural area where the cost of living is lower, then you are also going to have to lower your yearly income goal.

I am recommending that you push yourself. No doubt you are very motivated to begin with. Again, pushing yourself doesn't mean setting a ridiculous goal of making $200K in your first year of practice. Pushing yourself is foregoing the extra vacation your first year. It is going in on Fridays and sometimes working through the weekends. It is staying late sometimes. You will need to push the envelope to reach your financial goals. If you have a family or are married, this may be harder. It may require some sacrifices, just as completing grad school did. Remember, you are thinking about your future. Ultimately, making some sacrifices will be worth it. And if you work hard and save, you will be spending the holidays in Hawaii, rather than in Fargo.

If it is harder for you to set year-long goals, I suggest that you set quarterly goals. You will likely have to file taxes on a quarterly basis, so you will be aware of how much you are making quarterly because you'll need to take care of your books (again, I beseech you to please hand them off to your bookkeeper). So, a $25K quarter will land you in the realm of making $100K per year. That is a great quarter. As part of a good behavioral program for this, I highly recommend setting a reward for achieving your financial goals. For instance, I didn't take a real vacation last year, so I made my reward be a nice, week-long So Cal vacation (which I have already taken). This was a must, and trust me, I was looking forward to it all last year. Make sure to have a reasonable reward, as well. Don't pick something too cheap. An example of this would be meeting your financial goal and then joining the Jelly of the Month Club. Or going on a weekend hike. Unless you are hiking Mt. Fuji, that may not be something that you really look forward to. Choose a goal that is really valuable to you and is something that you will be excited to do. This will give you a better chance of meeting your financial goal—that is, according to the Premack principle. Isn't behavioral theory great?

While earning money is paramount, debt management completes the puzzle. This book will also explain how best to manage debt, and how debt can be a major motivator for you to be financially successful in your private practice. My close colleague, Dr. JD Friedman, wrote his dissertation on student-loan repayment and he has written a chapter that will help you with ideas about how to best tackle debt management. For those who have already graduated from a doctoral program in clinical psychology, or those who are current private practice psychologists, you might want to consider skipping the next few chapters, as you have already earned your black belts or gold stars. For those who are thinking about a career in clinical psychology, or are currently undergrad or grad students, please don't even think about putting down the book.

2

UNDERGRADUATE AND POST-UNDERGRADUATE EDUCATION

It is possible that some people who are reading this book have not started or completed undergraduate studies. So I will only say a few things about this. If you want to get into a doctoral program in clinical psychology, please read the book *Insider's Guide to Graduate Programs in Clinical and Counseling Psychology* by Dr. John Norcross. Read the book, because it has some great ideas for preparation. Now on to my advice. Do well. Do really well. Do not say, "I am going to take a semester off and relax." Work hard and try to attain at least decent grades. Decent meaning a 3.3 minimum. A 3.5 would be better. Of course, there is a stark contrast between a 3.3 at Harvard and a 3.3 at Washington State University. So if you are going to a less-critically acclaimed school you are going to have to do even better than your peers.

I would also recommend that you talk to a psychologist about their practice and what it is like for them being a psychologist. See if it interests you, and try to take a class on therapy or counseling. There should be a counseling center at your university. Consider talking to someone in the counseling center. Their time is free to you. Talk to them about therapy or psychology and what it is like. You don't have to be a psychology major to get into a doctoral program. I wasn't. But I did take a lot of psychology courses once I knew that I didn't want to be a History teacher or History professor. Take a lot of different courses in psychology and see what interests you. I remember finding Abnormal Psychology and the History of Psychology fascinating. There are always going to be individual interests in psychology, so take classes that are interesting to you, along with the required courses. There are prerequisite courses for doctoral programs in psychology.

Usually, the required courses include statistics, experimental psychology, abnormal psychology, developmental psychology, and personality theory. Each program has different requirements, so check into that before you apply to the program.

You will need to meet other requirements. Some of the less-competitive programs may accept a 3.0 or higher. But definitely do not slack off in your undergrad courses, particularly the ones in psychology. Some of the best programs are going to cut off at the 3.5 GPA. range or higher. The bottom line is that if you want to get into a doctoral program, you will need to take your undergrad classes very seriously. I have a section later on letters of recommendations, but take the letters seriously. The letters must be very good and need to come from former professors.

Consider doing research for university professors. Consider choosing a topic of research that interests you and that will correspond with a graduate program in clinical psychology. For instance, working in a statistics lab might not be the best background for applying for a doctoral program in clinical psychology, and might be better suited for research psychology. Some of the research might not be interesting to you, but consider the value of building the connection with the professor doing research. It is good to be doing things sometimes that don't interest us the most, if the activity will potentially help us in the future. I can remember going in for office hours when I was in undergrad. Building relationships with the faculty is really important, because they are going to be writing your recommendations. I'm not saying you need to be a sycophant, but let your professors know you and your interests, so that you stand out from the others. Participate in class so that they will know you and will see that you are engaged and interested. If you have a class that is important or meaningful to you in psychology, don't stay out partying the night before and don't show up for class hung over. Teachers will remember the kids who worked hard and participated in class, compared to those who didn't ask questions, didn't seem interested, and didn't participate. If there is a psychology club at your undergraduate institution, join, so you can talk with other like-minded people about psychology. I also recommend that you become very familiar with APA style of writing. Most of your undergrad courses will require you to write in APA style. This will be even more important to your work in graduate school. Consider studying the APA style manual. You may even have a course where you need to learn the manual. Learning the manual is an arduous and comprehensive process. There are many things in the manual that might not make sense, so ask your professors for help, if needed.

There are other ways to get your foot in the door with future clinical work. Strongly consider volunteering if you want to do clinical work. One idea is to volunteer at a homeless shelter for teens. That's what I did. It was an incredibly valuable experience. In particular, if you know that you want to do clinical work, make sure to get a little outside experience volunteering with a population that interests you. If you like working with developmentally delayed or autistic individuals, give the local clinic a call and offer your time. The worst thing that can happen is that they say no. The clinic will likely be happy to have some free labor. You can also try to volunteer at the school's counseling center. While you won't be counseling others, you can see what kind of work is going on, and you can chat with the clinicians there. University counseling centers are typically low-paying but somewhat high-profile jobs, not because of the pay, but because some clinicians have their summers off. If you can, talk to psychologists about their experiences that led them to counsel college students. Many of the counseling center jobs are highly competitive, so the individuals hired are usually highly qualified. This is also an opportunity to get recommendations for graduate school. Graduate schools are going to appreciate that you have some experience working in a clinical setting, even if it is for a few hours each week. This is an opportunity worth taking. If your school doesn't have a counseling center, consider volunteering at a nearby clinic.

Look for inspiration in your psych program. I found inspiration from Dr. Deborah Winter, an incredibly bright, engaging, warm, and well-published professor. She taught a History of Psychology course that was right up my alley, given that I was a History major. While I didn't exactly ace the class, I did learn a ton about something that was meaningful and interesting to me. The lectures and format were enthralling to me and provided a huge inspiration for me becoming a psychologist. You can find the same inspiration in your undergrad program. If you are in classes with professors that you don't like, or are in subjects that don't interest you, take different ones. Don't forget to challenge yourself. Just because the class is hard, doesn't mean that it is a bad class. I know this may sound scary, but you want to be thinking about what kind of psychology you want to practice in the future. If you are interested in research, consider doctoral programs that are strongly research based. If you are interested in psychological assessment (you are if you want to be financially successful), start thinking about programs that are strong in psychological assessment. Different institutions have different strengths, so keep that in mind before you apply to a doctoral program. Look into the different strengths and weaknesses that the programs have. It will be very possible that your interests in psychology will change once you are in graduate school. For me, I did not realize that I would be so interested in psychological testing when I was in undergraduate. I knew that I would be interested in domestic violence, school violence, and sports psychology, but I did not know that most of my clinical practice one day would be doing psychological testing. So keep in mind that your interests may change, as you will likely be inspired in many walks of psychology in grad school. Just be sure that you are applying to a program that has some of your current interests.

Summers will also be important. Be sure to work each summer. Or at least consider volunteering somewhere fulltime, because graduate schools are not only going to see a good scholastic record but also a good working record. I think it is probably fine to take your two-week vacation to Europe during a summer, but make sure that you do that before working—otherwise it is going to be difficult for you to find a job when you return. If necessary, start looking for work while you are still in your spring semester. If you are double-majoring and need to do coursework over the summer, that is also OK. Consider volunteering at an assisted living home or an area mental health clinic for a few hours each week if you intend to take classes over the summer. When thinking about jobs for the summer, don't take the easy way out. Well, make sure not to take the easy way out each summer. I think it is probably OK if you have a cakewalk job after your freshman year of college. If you want to be a waiter/waitress, that is probably fine. But if you do that for four years, graduate schools are going to recognize that you haven't attained any experience in psychology. While I taught tennis for two summers, I also did some volunteering with children and spent two summers working with children and adolescents in a day camp program. This day camp work was very psychologically based, as I was thrown into the world of child behavior problems and occasionally mitigating incompetent parents. So a strong vote here for doing some psychologically related work during your summers and not always taking the easy job.

The GRE

Not only do you not have to be a psychology major to get into a doctoral program, I think it actually can be an advantage to not be a psych major when you apply for grad schools. You may be seen as more well rounded. Yes, you will need to have the required psych classes, but majoring in another subject will not prevent you from getting in. Consider taking the GRE (Graduate Record Exam) prep course once you have finished undergrad (unless you feel that you are ready to take it during your senior year of undergrad). You can choose to do this over the summer. Or, if you have time, do it while you are in school. For me, I found that the GRE prep course greatly improved my scores. They teach you what you need to know on the exam, and they don't waste your time. They also give you practice tests and help you memorize huge vocabulary lists. This is an effective way to boost your score. When you are in undergrad, think about this course. I strongly advise you to take this course, especially if you are not well organized. You will need to take the GREs in the fall of your senior year (at the latest) if you are applying your senior year of college. If you are taking a year or two off, you will need to take them in the fall of the year that you are applying.

The GRE is a real challenge. For some, it is pretty easy. For others, it is a nightmare. Part of what is really difficult is that you will have to memorize a ton of new words. There is some good computer software out there that will help you with memorizing the words and working on your Greek and Latin roots. Please buy the stuff and work on it regularly. Learning new words isn't easy, and these are going to be words that you have heard maybe once or twice in your lifetime, if at all. The obscure words are going to show up in the exam and will have you scratching your head. Work on memorizing words so that you will be familiar with them. I worked on my vocab and greatly improved my verbal reasoning score. Some of the schools you will be applying for have cutoff scores, so the difference between a few points can be the difference between getting in and not getting accepted and having to apply the next year (and take the GREs again!). Talk about adding insult to injury.

If you are exceptionally good at math, read on. For those of you who aren't the best at math, like myself, continue the dialogue. You will have to work on your basic math skills. When is the last time you took a math class? For me, the last time was my senior year of high school, in which I took Calculus. My teacher was easy and I breezed by. But this is going to be harder. The GRE is known for having relatively easy content but really tricky ways of presenting it. For instance, you will get a lot of multiple-choice questions that will read "A and C" or "B and D," etc. They are going to try to trip you up by making you think twice about your answer. For those who tend to second-guess themselves on a multiple-choice format (definitely me), such a format can be nothing short of a complete and utter nightmare. You will need to go over Arithmetic, Geometry, and Algebra before you take the exam. If you think that you are "good" there, just do it anyway. Grad schools are very competitive and you want to give a full effort into getting into a decent school.

The thing that helps with taking the prep course is that there are instructors who want to help you. The instructor I had was gifted and did a good job with answering questions. It was good to have someone review with me and there was a classroom environment that was very helpful. You go to the class, and then you go home and work on what you have reviewed. The class will be lecture based, so some of the lectures might be more or less helpful. The keys here are to review some of the content where you might struggle and also learn some of the tricks that the instructors will teach you. Some of you who are reading this will figure, "This test is going to be a piece of cake." Were you the person who got a perfect score on the SAT (scholastic assessment test)? If so, OK, fine, move on to the next section. But for those of you who are more normal and don't ace every exam known to humankind (i.e., me), keep reading. This format of classroom learning and then reviewing what you have learned will provide structure to the process. I know that reviewing stuff at home is less than exciting. Who prefers spending their Friday or Saturday nights going over vocabulary lists or perhaps learning persuasive writing techniques? Fun, huh? Just do it. The party can wait until you are done. You will be happy that you have put in the time. After you do well on the exam, party. Working hard is worth a celebration.

Writing has always been a strength of mine, so I didn't really practice this too much. But in the prep courses, they will be able to greatly help you in this domain. They will show you samples of essays that are given different scores, depending on the content. Review the writing samples and see the differences in scores. Memorize what kind of essays illustrate a high GRE score. Don't worry about writing something creative or masterful. Just memorize what you need to score well. That's all you need to do. I ended up doing well on the writing section, so that boosted my chances of getting into grad school. I think that the grad schools weigh this section highly because you are going to need to be a good writer when you are in a clinical psychology program. You are going to be doing a ton of report writing and you will need to be a solid writer. So if you have a lot of work to do in this domain, really put in the effort. Hire a tutor if you have some major writing problems or if you have not done well in English or college-level writing courses. The analytical writing section has two parts which require you to analyze an issue and analyze an argument. The "analyze an issue" essay will require you to evaluate the issue, understand its complexities, and state an argument, with evidence to support your argument. The "analyze an argument" essay asks you to evaluate an argument based on specific parameters and to consider the logic behind the argument, rather than agreeing or disagreeing with the argument. The GRE class will help you to better understand how each of these essays are scored and what you will need to present in order to attain a high score. Basically, the essays are tasks of persuasive writing and complex thinking.

But time-management is also important for the essays, as 30 minutes are allotted for each essay. It will be important for you to do a good pre-write and to work through a draft of your argument. Make sure to check your work at the end, as a few errors won't lower your score, but persistent errors will negatively affect your score. Again, the GRE class can greatly help you prepare for these essays.

In 2011, they revised the GRE to create a newer, friendlier design that includes having a calculator on the computer screen. It also includes having questions that are more similar to real-life situations. Apparently, they have noted that there will be a greater emphasis on what they consider to be "higher level cognitive skills." They are no longer having antonyms or analogies, which means that you are not going to have to work quite as hard on memorizing those vocabulary words. You are going to need to know about critical reasoning questions by reading passages and then answering questions about them. For more information, visit the GRE website at www.ets.org.

Recommendations

Once you are out of college, you are bound to have some accolades. Perhaps you were not valedictorian, you did not win award after award, and you did not win rave reviews from all of your professors. Or maybe you did. Likely, you did well and have some good recommendations. Hopefully, you impressed some professors. Hold onto those recommendations, because you never know when you are going to need them. Take, for instance, university teaching positions. Usually when you are applying for teaching positions, the university will call at least someone for your recommendations. I hardly need to tell you how important it is to keep in touch with these people who are on your list of recommendations because you never know when they are going to be called. And please, choose people on your recommendations list who will give you a glowing recommendation. Choose people who are great humans, who do interesting work, whom you would introduce to your family. I'm talking about former professors and former supervisors. I'm not talking about friends or relatives. Perhaps I am stating the obvious here. I was fortunate enough to have a diverse group who will give me recommendations. The people on my list are some truly interesting and exceptional humans, whose who are either gifted clinicians or gifted professors. They are all passionate, articulate individuals who profoundly influenced my graduate school career. They are the kind of people that make me smile when I think about them. I'm just trying to drive home a point here that you never know how significant your references may be.

Applying to Graduate School

It is essential to have some clever and well-written essays on why you would make a good psychologist. Really spend some time here and think about what to say and what not to say. Do not say that you know everything. Try not to indicate something trite like "I have always wanted to be a psychologist, since I was a kid." No, really, you wanted to be a psychologist when you were a kid? Not impossible but unlikely. Think about creative ways to convey your message. Think about influences or points of inspiration. For me, it was teaching tennis with kids when I was in college. I related well with the kids and was able to connect with the parents. I learned a ton about family dynamics by teaching tennis and about the problems that children and families face. Something like that would suffice. Do not talk about how you want to save the world and how you are going to be the best psychologist ever. Try not to have a narcissistic vein to your essays. Really think hard about ways that you have been inspired. It is OK to be funny and witty with these essays.

You might be asked to write an essay about overcoming odds or fighting through a difficult situation/adversity. I am sure that at some point in your life you have had a difficult situation. Think about this really hard and write down several situations. Find the situation that is most applicable to psychology. Think about a creative way to work through this question. Do not give them the standard response. At the same time, don't say anything unacademic or weird, either. You don't want to be seen as a slacker. If you have overcome a physical challenge, or suffered a personal loss, these may be good choices. If it is not too painful, adding humor to the situation may be helpful. Writing style is another important issue. Do not write your essay in a flowery style.

Use language that is consistent with APA style. When I was teaching graduate school a few years back, I was amazed at how many students didn't write in APA style. Really work on this if you haven't had much practice. Some schools will really hammer APA style, and this is just something that you are going to have to be very comfortable with in grad school. If you don't have undergrad experience with APA style, you need to pick up the APA manual and read it cover to cover. It is tedious to do something like that, but it could make a difference. Getting into a doctoral program is not easy. You are going to want every advantage.

Graduate school essays may also ask you about your strengths and weaknesses. Consider what your best friend would say about you. How would he/she describe you? Make sure that your best friend would take a blunt or honest approach to this. You may want to write down some things and then come up with the best approach. Really use some introspection. Look inside and think about your positive and negative points. If you are thinking that you really don't have any negative points, think again. And then get back to the project. Or ask someone close to you what you can work on. Maybe your parents would have some good info here. Or maybe not. Be as honest as you can. But don't make yourself look like you have a ton of flaws . . . just make it look like you are human, with things that you can always work on. Discuss what you have done to overcome the weaknesses or flaws. Avoid trite statements. Examples include that you are good at working with and reading people. Do not say that in your essay. If you do indicate that you are good at working with people, say so in a different way and offer many examples as evidence.

The essays prompts are likely going to ask you about what draws you to the specific clinical program. Yes, if you are applying to many schools this means that you are going to need to tailor your essay to each specific program. If there is a faculty member that you know about or are interested in doing clinical work or research with, indicate this and why you want to work with them. Think about what attracts you to the program. Maybe it is the therapeutic orientation of specific core faculty, or maybe it's the courses offered in the program. Finally, make sure to edit your essays very carefully. Have another person who is applying to graduate school in psychology edit your essay. You could also take your essay to a university writing center whose staff will edit your essay for free. Free is always good. There should be no mistakes, grammatical errors, or typographical errors in your essays, so read them over again and again. You want perfection here, and good graduate schools will expect nothing short of a wonderfully written essay. No pressure, of course.

You may want to take a year off to work or to gain experience. I ended up taking a year off after my undergrad to work for a low-income mental health clinic. Working with foster youth definitely cemented my interest in psychology. I was afforded the opportunity while working at the clinic to gain experience from Master's-level therapists who taught me about treatment plans, behavior modification, and other topics in clinical psychology. In my year at the clinic, I learned considerably more about therapy and treatment than I did during my undergraduate psychology classes. I recommend that you take a year to work in some field of clinical psychology. The year that I worked I was basically taking orders from therapists on what to do with the kids and what not to do. This was a valuable experience. If you have an exceptional resume or have already a good deal of experience working in the mental health field, you may not need to do this for graduate school. I can be certain that grad schools liked that I had spent the year working in the field and not bartending. So that is what not to do . . . don't take the year off to bartend, hostess, travel, or do other things that will not improve your resume. You want to only do things that will improve your chances of getting into grad school. These doctoral programs are competitive, and I found myself very fortunate to get into the program that I wanted.

Taking a year off is a way that you can strengthen your application for graduate schools. If you don't feel that you are the strongest applicant for doctoral programs, having a year of clinical experience is something that graduate schools will value. There are tons of opportunities for those who want to have a job that is related to clinical psychology out of undergraduate. Most of these jobs are not well paying, but looking toward the big picture and getting accepted into a doctoral program, it is totally worth having one year where you aren't making good money. One year of earning low wages at a community mental health setting is completely worth it, if you have 30 years of making good money in a financially successful private practice. APA has noted that there is a wide array of jobs for those who are psychology majors. Psychology's dazzling array of careers. *APA Monitor on Psychology, 32*(2). Fowler (2001) writes,

> Studying psychology at the bachelor's level has always been considered a good preparation for working with people in a variety of fields. Although there are few jobs available in psychology for college graduates, they find jobs in many varied fields including administration, public affairs, business, sales, health, education, journalism and computer programming. Until recently, going to graduate school seemed to narrow rather than expand the variety of available jobs. The young psychologists profiled in this *Monitor* demonstrate that that is no longer the case.

Fowler (2001) also added that among those with college degrees, psychology is the third-fastest growing field—meaning that there are plenty of opportunities for those who have undergrad degrees in psychology. More recent research from APA indicates that psychology is the third most popular undergraduate field, as of 2008 (http://www.apa.org/careers/resources/guides/careers.aspx). APA also has career resources on their website (http://www.apa.org/careers/resources/guides/careers.aspx). They explain,

> As has long been true, opportunities in psychology for those with graduate degrees will be more plentiful and at a higher level than for those with undergraduate degrees. An undergraduate degree remains excellent preparation for continued graduate work in psychology or in another field, such as business, medicine or computer science. Many employers are interested in the skills that psychology majors bring to collecting, analyzing and interpreting data and their experience with statistics and experimental design.

Also note that knowledge attained for an undergraduate degree in psychology will help aid in finding employment in a variety of settings. APA explains,

> The study of psychology at the bachelor's degree level is also good preparation for many other professions. In 2008, 5 percent of recipients of

bachelor's degrees in psychology were working in psychology or in an occupation related to psychology. Of the small proportion working in psychology, over 80 percent were in educational settings, broadly defined. People with bachelor's degrees in psychology often possess good research and writing skills, are good problem solvers and have well-developed, higher level thinking abilities when it comes to analyzing, synthesizing and evaluating information. Many find jobs in administrative support, public affairs, education, business, sales, service industries, health, the biological sciences and computer programming. They may also work as employment counselors, correction counselor trainees, interviewers, personnel analysts, probation officers and writers. (http://www.apa.org/careers/resources/guides/careers.aspx)

Now I want to be clear. I am not suggesting that you start your career once you have completed your undergrad degree. What I am stating is that you will have opportunities to work in the field for one to two years following your degree. Working in the field and applying the knowledge in psychology attained from undergrad will make you a stronger applicant for doctoral programs. Grad schools are going to value you working as a domestic violence advocate, a preschool teacher, line staff at a hospital, or in other psychology-related fields. This will also be an opportunity to write about the value of what you have been doing in your graduate school essays.

When you are preparing for graduate school, think about the schools that would be a good fit for you. Do you want to do research or do you want to do clinical work? If you want to do research, choose a research driven school. If you want to improve your clinical work, apply to schools that are strong in that domain. Norcross's book has a ton of great information about research schools vs. clinical schools. I would not recommend applying to long-shot schools. For instance, some schools, such as Yale, require at least two years of research experience for their doctoral program. I definitely did not fit that mold and I couldn't have gotten in with my undergrad grades and test scores. A little introspection here will mean not applying to ridiculously competitive schools, unless you are the next Einstein. Maybe you are. Then do it. But don't shortchange yourself, either. Apply to some schools where you might not fit the criteria. You never know what they are looking for. Maybe they are looking to find a student that is a bit outside of their comfort zone. You might get in and find that you love the place.

You want to apply to only APA-approved programs. Some states will not accept non-APA approved programs. Because licensure in each state is varied, only apply to APA-approved programs. If the program is not APA approved, usually there is a good reason why that is the case. Also, if you want to teach someday, many positions will only accept candidates who have graduated from APA-approved programs. If a program has been APA approved and has lost APA approval, do not apply to the program. Usually those programs do not have the rigor or acclaim that other programs have. I have heard horror stories from colleagues who were in APA-approved programs that lost APA approval while they were in the program and they were already knee-deep in their program and had to complete it. Then they tried to find jobs or tried to get licensed and they couldn't, because their institution was no longer APA approved. Bottom line, you want to be sure that the program that you are applying to is not a concern for losing APA approval. Check and see if they have ever lost APA approval before you apply to the program. Do not apply to online programs, as most of them are not APA accredited. I don't care if they are more convenient; you are building for your future here! You want to go to the best program that you can.

Do not just apply for schools in your region, either. I grew up in the Pacific Northwest and I applied to schools all across the United States. Applying to schools is a bit like throwing dice and hoping that they land on red, so really consider applying to a variety of schools. I knew that ultimately I wanted to be on the West Coast and I was fortunate enough to get into a school in San Diego. But, honestly, you do not know where you will be accepted, so don't limit yourself by only applying to local schools. If you don't get into those schools you will have to wait another year and apply again . . . and could have the same thing happen the following year. Remember that if you apply for a program in a section of the United States that you are not thrilled about, you will only be living there for five years. This will not be your entire life.

It might be well worth going there, and you may also find that you like it more than you anticipate.

Relationships and Families

If you have a family, moving to another part of the United States becomes more complicated. This can be a tricky situation, because your spouse or partner might already be earning good money in your current location. Remember that this book is about starting and maintaining a financially successful private practice in clinical psych, but money is money. If you have a partner who is supportive both emotionally and financially, you might want to consider the financial impact of moving from New York to LA and uprooting the family and your partner's well-paying job. You might want to do some math here and decide whether moving would be worth it. This also depends on the amount of student loans that you will need to take out. For instance, if you need to take out $80K in loans and your husband or wife is making $80K per year, there is a huge difference between doing that and not taking out any loans because your husband or wife makes $150K per year. These are all things to consider.

For those who are in relationships and long-term relationships, it will take a lot of communicating when you are applying for graduate school programs. I can remember when I was applying for graduate school programs at the ripe old age of 22. I knew that I wanted to be a clinical psychologist. My girlfriend at the time was not so sure that I was choosing the right program, and there was nothing that I could do to change her mind. She wanted the best for me. She thought that it would be best to have another year or to have an internship in clinical psych (which typically doesn't really exist for those who only have an undergrad degree). While part of me was scared to begin a doctoral program, most of me felt ready. We were both doing somewhat different things at the time, as she wanted to teach tennis abroad and I had already spent three years teaching tennis. I wanted a new, more academic challenge. So we were clearly both not in the same place mentally. If you are in a relationship when you are applying for graduate schools, this is something that you both need to talk about. If your partner or boyfriend/girlfriend has a good job and is stable, they may not want to move across country. Depending on the state of your relationship, your decision to move away may be a deal-breaker. I don't want to tell you that you should break up your relationship if you are planning on moving across country to a doctoral program. I am saying that individuation is healthy and choosing your own path is the way to being financially successful. There might be a program or job for your partner where you are planning on moving. Or there might not. If you are in a long-term relationship and are applying to a doctoral program out of state, I recommend talking to your partner early and communicating freely about this subject. The last thing you want to do to them is tell them unexpectedly that you are moving away.

If you are considering applying to graduate school and you have small children, you might want to consider waiting a few years until they are older and can better cope with the move. You also might want to wait a few years because of the irreplaceable value of spending time with your children. I think that you will know what is best for you and your children, and what the family can cope with. Moving is tough on children, whether they are four or 14. You can't place a value on watching your children grow up, so if you are a stay at home mother or father, that is something to consider as well. Depending on the age of your children, it will be important for you to communicate early to them about moving and what that might entail. Doctoral programs in psychology are not typically part-time—especially those that are APA accredited. You want to consider the value of spending time with your children if you are applying for graduate school programs. Some mothers and fathers are perfectly fine with having babysitters or *au pairs* while their children are young, while others wouldn't dream of that being an option. You know what is best in this domain. It is a lot to consider if you are married with children. If that is the case, I would not recommend living somewhere else, away from your family. I think that could be a disconnecting option for the family. If you are considering that option, that indicates that things might not be the best in your family. Balancing the needs of your family and the requirements of grad school might be a laborious process, one you will have to work out with your partner and your family's support system (which may include preschool, babysitters, grandparents, and daycare). If you have a family, it is a difficult process going through graduate school. One might argue that there is really never a great time to go through graduate school if you already have children—especially, if the children are young and require more careful attention and supervision.

It is imperative to visit the graduate schools where you are applying. Only visit the schools that have accepted you or that have wait-listed you. Visit the campuses and visualize yourself there. Some may seem like an inadequate fit. Try not to choose those schools, unless you were not accepted by other schools. If the school feels like a good fit, go there. You should visit each school that you are seriously considering. Budget for the trips, or if you need to, ask your parents for some financial help. Explain that the trips are really investing in your future. Hopefully, they will buy your sales pitch. These trips are not cheap. For instance, if you do three visits, you will likely need to budget for $1,000 at the least for each trip, including airfare, hotel, food, rental cars, and other expenses. Try to make some contact with the department that you are applying to and you can ask for a tour. They will be able to show you the classrooms and the environment that you will be in for the next five-plus years. You may also be able to set up short visits with faculty. When you are doing these visits, dress up and dress conservatively. Try to get a feel for the faculty. Think about how they react to you, as some may appear as friendly and others may feel brusque or cold. You can also email a student representative and talk to them about their experience in the program. Also consider contacting random students in the program about their experience, as the student representative may not be quite as candid regarding their experience.

References

American Psychological Association. Psychology a popular career. Retrieved from http://www.apa.org/careers/resources/guides/careers.aspx

Fowler, R. (2001). Psychology's dazzling array of careers. *APA Monitor on Psychology, 32*(2), 9. Retrieved from http://www.apa.org/monitor/feb01/rc.aspx

3

ON STUDENT LOANS

Dr. JD Friedman

Money is a singular thing. It ranks with love as man's greatest source of joy. And with death as his greatest source of anxiety.

John Kenneth Galbraith

Thinking about Your Financial Thinking

If you've learned any single lesson from Dr. Bargreen thus far, I hope it is this: starting a financially successful practice in psychology begins *before* you even get to graduate school. Ideally, it starts with shrewd financial planning for your graduate education and training, combined with a blueprint and strategy for repaying student loans. The correct blueprint has become even more important over the past 15 years, during which time accumulating loan totals in excess of $100K has become commonplace. Meanwhile, during the same period, psychologists' incomes have largely stagnated or declined, as has federal funding for practitioners. So it is essential to ask yourself, "How much student loan debt is too much?" Have you given enough thought to that question before embarking upon the marathon that is graduate school, not to mention the half-marathon necessary in most states to obtain a license? After all, as Dr. Bargreen details, building and maintaining a financially profitable practice requires overhead costs of time, labor, and capital. If you aren't careful, a huge monthly student loan payment can become a proverbial white elephant hanging out with your patients in the waiting room.

You see, psychologists today live and work in an increasingly competitive marketplace in which Master's-level non-psychologists and red tape from insurance companies are squeezing market share and holding down hourly rates. Moreover, many students enter psychology programs with insufficient knowledge and/or experience with personal finance, let alone with the economics of small business development. Although in recent years the American Psychological Association (APA) has begun to advocate for the inclusion of practice management and personal finance into psychology graduate school curricula, the vast majority of graduate psychology programs have yet to make the transition. It doesn't take much of a leap to suggest, therefore, that a substantial number of entering, and even graduating, students lack a full appreciation for what it means to repay $100,000 in student loans, let alone $150,000, or even $200,000.

This is unsurprising. For decades, mainstream thinking in the United States has groomed young people to think of educational debt as plain old "good debt," end of story. That mindset, meanwhile, has combined with legislative changes making student loans more abundant and accessible. As a result, students over the past 20 years have taken out historic sums of so-called good debt, perhaps without thinking through the full implications of that debt. In fact, the sum total for outstanding student loans in the United States has topped the $1 trillion mark. That's right, one trillion bucks of "good debt." Thus, I can't emphasize it enough: while educational debt often can be utilized to pave the way for personal and professional advancement, it still is vitally important to consider cost-benefit analyses that draw a line past which educational debt becomes "bad debt."

Simply stated, in the present age, wearing financial blinders is reckless, while developing your financial chops has become increasingly important. This remains particularly true for practitioners in psychology, who cannot count on the more lavish salaries awaiting fresh graduates from medical, law, and business schools. Between 1997 and 2005 alone, the median amount of loans among psychology graduates with a clinical PsyD increased by almost 90 percent to $100,000, and nearly 68 percent completed their training with more than $75,000 to repay. Meanwhile, psychology graduates with a clinical PhD assumed over 50 percent more loans during the same six years, and over one-fourth also finished with student debt exceeding $75,000. Without self-reflecting to determine how much is too much student loan debt, you risk following in the footsteps of many students who entered their doctoral psychology program as neophytes about personal finance and its relationship with personal and professional aspirations. Thus, although it may be outside your comfort zone, you ought to begin first by mapping how to finance your education in a cost-effective manner. Indeed, Dr. Bargreen and I are not alone in this viewpoint.

My colleague Jessica Dolgan, PsyD, a highly successful, entrepreneurial private practitioner based in Denver, CO, is an authority on business issues facing private practitioners. In her doctoral dissertation, she cited vocational studies asserting that psychologists' interests continue to revolve primarily around social and investigative pursuits, and rarely in the direction of enterprising interests. According to Dolgan, these vocational studies suggest that, generally speaking, "not only do [psychologists] not know how to do finance but they also have little interest in doing so" (Dolgan, 2004, p. 31). Concerning this state of affairs, she concludes, "Those therapists seeking to retain a position in the marketplace have learned that understanding business practices is not a negotiable skill" (p. 32).

In an article entitled "It's Time To Do Something About Our Future," former president of the American Psychological Association, Stanley Graham, PhD, lamented the state of psychology for its newest members, calling attention to alarming economic trends working against the interests of burgeoning practitioners. Graham (2008) emphasized that increasing numbers of students are completing pre-doctoral requirements with substantial debt. Then, upon graduating, they are finding insufficient near-term financial opportunities due to limited practice rights and burdensome postdoctoral requirements for licensure. Graham also expressed his dismay that demand for quality accredited training opportunities increasingly outweighs supply, and noted that many new graduates are left without institutional support to help them gain a foothold in their careers and, therefore, their financial lives. What's more, Graham published his article in February 2008, which means that his concerns were conveyed at a time *preceding* the Great Recession, whose effects are still with all of us today.

Yet the more things change, the more they seemingly remain the same. Just recently, I was speaking with some of the psychology interns whom I supervise about their student loans and loan repayment. One matter-of-factly acknowledged that she will owe $250,000 upon completing her degree; another stated, without evident dissonance, that she just pretends her voluminous loans don't exist, based upon an assumption she will qualify for loan reimbursement in the future; a third relayed the story of a friend, lacking subsidized loans, who pays the accumulating interest on loans with, you guessed it, more student loans. Indeed, studies demonstrate that students in general exhibit what is known as an optimism bias in their perceptions and expectations about repaying their student loans. They underestimate the difficulties that can arise from repaying educational debts, while overestimating the amount of money they will make following graduation. Simply put, many newcomers to the field assume, and often are influenced by school administrators, parents, and friends, that it'll all work out in the end. In most cases, it probably will all work out in the end. However, don't lose sight of the fact that there's also a lot of "in the middle" to get through before you can get to that end. Or, to quote a refrain from a popular song by the band Stealers Wheel, "clowns to the left of me, jokers to the right, here I am, stuck in the middle with you."

I, too, am "stuck in the middle" of a 30-year, six-figure repayment, with attendant clowns and jokers, and as such can vouch for the powerful influence of an optimism bias. Looking back, I believe I was naïve about money and debt, as well as overly idealistic in my expectations about what graduating with a doctorate in clinical psychology might entail. To my credit and yours, I was not driven by a lust for money, but rather by a desire to find a fulfilling career that would be of service to others. Yet to my detriment, I also had very little perspective on fiscal matters and lacked a necessary analytic and strategic mindset for evaluating money's role in my future plans. And why not: I completed a bachelor's degree from a very expensive, prestigious university, yet with the good fortune to graduate with only a few grand in student loans. Good fortune? No doubt. Reality? Hardly. Trust me when I say seeing a monthly bill of $50 for undergraduate loans was not particularly influential in my thinking about taking student loans for graduate school.

The world literally was my oyster, as it may be yours as well, and that's all the more reason to take your time to comprehensively evaluate the wisdom and practicality of paying for an advanced degree in the field of psychology. Back then, I thought I had done just that, because I sought guidance from some very successful people, including attorneys, businessmen, and practicing psychologists. Almost universally, they reiterated the mantra about educational debt being "good debt," while espousing gauzy, well-intentioned platitudes to the effect that, "If you love what you do the money will be there." Sounds nice, and I've come to believe there's value and truth to that sentiment. However, I've also learned that value is very much relative. Put another way by the late William F. Buckley, "Idealism is fine, but as it approaches reality, the costs become prohibitive." Moreover, people grow and change over time, while their experiences help to guide their direction and shape their interests. It is asking a lot to assume on blind faith that you will love working in a field, and therefore magnetically attract ample compensation, years prior to working professionally in that same field.

In other words, it behooves you to calculate the "opportunity costs" associated with your various options for pursuing your educational and professional goals. In this regard, I came to understand only after the fact just how much taking out loans is not merely about taking out the loans themselves. Taking out loans is about forgoing various alternative options. For example, it is reasonable to conclude that by completing an expensive degree in psychology, you are firmly committing yourself to a niche occupation. In doing so, you also forgo income that you could have earned had you chosen to work during the same "starving" graduate school years.

Let's consider a hypothetical scenario to illustrate the point. Assume you spend an expected five years pursuing a doctorate in graduate school and accumulate $125,000 in student loans. First, you end up on the hook for that sum—the principal—before interest ever kicks in. Second, by forgoing a modest annual income that would have netted you, say, $15,000 per year after taxes and life expenses, the numeric cost of your five-year education actually winds up in the neighborhood of $200,000. A real-life example also portrays this principle. Prior to switching gears to take on a tour of graduate school duty, a friend from my graduate program was employed in a $100,000 per year sales position. Her doctorate in clinical psychology ultimately cost her around

$150,000. Accounting for the roughly $30,000 per year she could have continued to take home from her sales job after taxes and life expenses, and you'll see that the opportunity-cost of her education ended up being upwards of $300,000. If someone asked you what you would do with $150,000 to spend, let alone $300,000 to spend/retain, what do you think you would choose?

In addition to inadequately understanding the opportunity costs associated with my graduate school ambitions, I also was enamored with the notion of becoming a "doctor." I sometimes fantasized about the many positives I expected the title would accrue to me. In particular, I imagined it would benefit my ego, social stature, dating life, and bank account. Today, Dr. Bargreen and I both can attest that earning a doctorate is a satisfying feeling; it's an achievement that no one can take away from you. It is particularly gratifying in light of how relentlessly stressful it was to traverse the graduate-school marathon. We also can share that holding the title of "doctor" can be exciting and initially was novel, but the excitement quickly wears off. Have you checked in with yourself to make sure you are giving proper but not excessive weight to imagined and/or idealized perks? While reflecting upon this question, I implore you to keep in mind a simple point: it is increasingly the case that a career in psychology requires a rather luxurious price tag for admission, but the perks are not as grand as they used to be. So when you consider the upside of becoming a "doctor," keep in mind that during and probably for a while after graduate school, you are likely to be a doctor of ramen noodles. Caviar, if it ever is served, will not be on the menu for quite some time.

Given the above, it probably will not come as a surprise that I wish I knew as a student what I now know as a professional. If afforded an accounting reset button, I would have approached financing my education very differently. That said, my graduate school cohort did not have the benefit of Dr. Bargreen's practical guidance. We began our graduate education in 2002–2003, a time when the national economy was not stuck in neutral. Back then, the economy was surging forward on the mirage of what turned out to be the housing bubble. Moreover, back when Dr. Bargreen and I passed through graduate school, there was no research whatsoever about student loans and their effects upon practicing psychologists. You, on the other hand, are both fortunate and smart to read Dr. Bargreen's book in order to prepare yourself to blueprint your future as a clinician. You have the opportunity to make shrewder and better-informed decisions about financing your education than were those before you. You are in position to maximize the value and overall profitability of your education and training, such that it will work in your favor and not in favor of that elephant in the waiting room.

Student Loan Repayment: The Experience

In addition to personal and anecdotal experiences, I also completed a doctoral dissertation on the issue of high-volume student loan repayment among early career psychologists. My dissertation, entitled "Student Loan Repayment: The Experience of Early Career Psychologists" (Friedman, J., 2008), confirmed that psychologists repaying high levels of student loans relative to their earnings can expect to encounter a number of hidden costs and sacrifices during the initial repayment years. In other words, paying back student loans impacted the lives of the participants in my study in many ways they were unprepared to face, which caused them chronic stress, and even outright suffering.

My study employed a qualitative research design in order to find real-world answers to questions about the participants' life experiences, most notably: What kinds of stressors are associated with loan repayment, and how do fledgling psychologists experience these stressors? In what ways do financial limitations associated with loan repayment influence early career psychologists' personal and professional aspirations? In what ways can loan repayment influence new psychologists' satisfaction with enjoyment of their work? Although the results cannot be said to generalize to all early career psychologists, the lessons and inferences drawn from my study can help you better understand what the experience of loan repayment might be like for you, and perhaps where to draw the line. Thinking through these lessons can help guide you to make tailored decisions that best suit your goals. In other words, think of what follows as a chance for you to imagine what a "virtual reality" might look like for your future as a new psychologist were you to have substantial loans to pay back.

The participants in my study were all psychologists licensed between one to six years, ranging in age from 27 to 55, from varied financial, cultural, ethnic, and racial backgrounds. Each practiced in diverse professional roles across a wide geographic area covering seven states. The average participant was 35.5 years old, female, licensed for slightly more than two years, and repaying loans for approximately three and a half years. The average participant originally accrued $148,700 in educational debt, and at the time of our qualitative interview still owed an average of $142,000, with a monthly payment of $830 and a monthly net income of $3,800. That's $3,800 *after taxes,* so when one of your professors inevitably announces that "any of you who are here to get rich is in the wrong field," *believe him/her.* Specific figures are detailed for each participant in the table below.

Although opinions differ as to what constitutes reasonable versus risky amounts of student loan borrowing, the results of a national student loan survey from 2002 reported that feelings of burden associated with loan repayment increase incrementally, beginning with those owing between 7 to 11 percent, followed by those owing between 12 to

Table 3.1 Participants' Financial Demographics*

PARTICIPANT	TIME WITH LICENSE	TIME REPAYING LOANS (TERM OF REPAYMENT)	ORIGINAL LOAN AMOUNT	LOAN AMOUNT REMAINING	MONTHLY LOAN PAYMENT	NET MONTHLY INCOME	DEBT-TO-INCOME RATIO**
1	1.5 years	7 years (30)	$120,000	$130,000	$1,050	$4,000#	26.00%
2	2.5 years	1.25 years (30)	$214,000	$225,000	$850	$5,000#	17.00%
3	1.5 years	2 years (30)	$180,000	$170,000	$500	$2,000	25.00%
4	1.0 years	2 years (30)	$150,000	$130,000	$550	$2,500#	22.00%
5	1.0 years	2 years (30)	$175,000	$173,000	$900	$2,900	31.00%
6	2.0 years	3.5 years (10)	$97,000	$50,000	$1,000	$6,000#	17.00%
7	2.0 years	4 years (30)	$150,000	$200,000	$650	$3,000	22.00%
8	0.75 years	1.25 years (30)	$200,000	$215,500	$700	$3,000	23.00%
9	4.0 years	5 years (10)	$80,000	$56,625	$1,300	$5,600#	23.00%
10	5.0 years	8 years (30)	$121,000	$70,000	$800	$4,000	20.00%

* Figures shown are best estimates by participant

** Rounded to the nearest full percentage

Combined net monthly family income

16 percent, and peaking with those exceeding the 17 percent threshold (Baum & O'Malley, 2003). Thus, as you are reading, and hopefully pondering the question "How much student debt is too much?," it is important to keep in mind that my dissertation focused on the most-indebted cohort of early career psychologists.

Indeed, the debt-to-income ratio of 17 percent and above has been associated with the highest degree of financial strain. Broadly defined, financial strain describes various combinations of potentially harmful stressors that can accumulate and wreak havoc in one's life. Of note, the experience of financial strain can harm peoples' self-esteem, disrupt marriages and intimate relationships, increase levels of anxiety and depression, increase incidences of physical illness, and diminish over-all levels of reported life-satisfaction. Financial strain can derive from external life pressures associated with one's economic realities, as well as self-critical beliefs and negative feelings originating with an individual's perceived difficulties in meeting his or her economic and/or material desires. Experienced financial strain was evident in myriad ways for each of the participants in my study, who on average reported a 22 percent debt-to-income ratio. Every participant reported a minimum debt-to-income ratio of at least 17 percent, meaning for every $100 dollars they took home after taxes, they owed at least $17 toward student loans.

How might these percentages look as a proportion of one's overall life expenses? The following graph breaks it down to provide a visual representation of what a 22 percent debt-to-income ratio could look like as a portion of your economic world.

Admittedly, the impact of any given debt-to-income ratio will vary depending on a person's individual circumstances, including financial support provided by one's family, preexisting savings and/or equity, differences in cost of living and taxation by state and by region, as well the impact of macroeconomic trends upon one's life (i.e., inflation in everyday products and services, fluctuations in the price of gasoline, etc.). Notwithstanding individual differences, the graph represents a plausible, if not a conservative, estimate of life expenses and the Pac-man-like chunk that student loans can consume.

The reported experiences detailed by the psychologists in my study were equally instructive as well as cautionary. If the graph can be

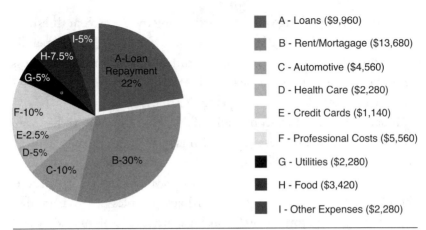

A - Loans ($9,960)

B - Rent/Mortagage ($13,680)

C - Automotive ($4,560)

D - Health Care ($2,280)

E - Credit Cards ($1,140)

F - Professional Costs ($5,560)

G - Utilities ($2,280)

H - Food ($3,420)

I - Other Expenses ($2,280)

Figure 3.1 All Figures Estimated Based Upon Average Participant Net Income $45,600

said to represent the skeletal frame of a highly indebted psychologist's economic life, the participants' oft-poignant narratives may be said to constitute the central nervous system of their economic life. To wit, results from my study revealed 14 discrete themes related to the participating psychologists' experience of student loan repayment. The themes are organized into four categories, each constituting a core, meaningful domain of their endorsed and elaborated experience of loan repayment. The core categories were: (1) Participants' Experience of Financial Strain, (2) Participants' Experience of Rewards and Sacrifices, (3) Participants' Experience of Loans and Education as Investment, and (4) Participants' Experience of Resilience and Growth.

In the first category, the psychologists reported an experience of acute financial strain that was most severe leading up to and during their preliminary repayment, a period concurrent with the time of their obtaining initial licensure. This strain typically included intense anxiety, fear, chronic worrying, and even grief-like experiences. I recall that participant #5 appeared virtually wounded with dismay when discussing her regrets and constant struggles to maintain hope and optimism that she eventually would be free of repaying her loans. She described herself being tied to a substantial monthly bill as akin to feeling as if she was "in bondage." She further stated, "It's been an incredible burden . . . a heavy weight, it's a monkey on my back all the time, just all the time."

Although the exact emotional experiences at moments of heightened strain varied from one participant to another, their stressful emotional states linked with negative self-appraisals, a nagging experience of ongoing self-criticisms and chronic rumination about their financial health and future. Participant #2 spoke about living in a "state of fear" and a "state of denial" wherein, "You just let the interest accrue and pray that one day you're going to be able to pay it off." Her feelings also extended to guilt and remorse that her husband, who was debt free prior to their marriage, "is stuck with it too." In a similar vein, participant #7 remarked, "I've been very independent and I've wanted to be able to be a partner in a marriage, not a dependent on somebody. So sometimes I feel guilty that [my husband is] supporting me so much." Participant #10 reported feelings of "anger at myself" when talking with others about her loans; she noted memorably, "Sometimes I feel like a horse in the reins."

The psychologists in my study also described various concrete, tangible approaches they used to cope with the stress associated with their loan repayment. They used their knowledge of psychology to their benefit. Several emphasized the importance of establishing a support network, and they identified helpful coping methods commonly associated with cognitive-behavioral psychology. Effective techniques for managing the rigors of financial strain included positively reframing the repayment experience, using affirmative and motivational self-talk, and scrutinizing often punishingly self-critical beliefs and/or distortions. Some participants derived meaning and clarity of purpose through personal initiative, such as establishing concrete plans and strategies for repayment, or by mentoring students considering taking loans for school.

In the second emergent category, the participating psychologists reported dissatisfactions with their salaries and expressed concerns about diminishing earning potential for practitioners in an era increasingly squeezed by managed care restrictions. Participant #4 described difficulties in loan repayment that interfered in his attempts at growing his fledgling private practice. He noted, "I'd like to advertise more than I do, but I'm prohibited by the amount of money. [My loans] factor in a lot when I think about advertising . . . I feel like I have to spend my money as little as possible and as wisely as possible."

One way of understanding the participants' dissatisfaction with their compensation is to view their experience through the prism of what's known as "equity theory." According to equity theory, people's satisfaction with their pay is a byproduct partially determined by their perceptions and social comparisons. In particular, they consider a ratio of so-called inputs, namely their efforts, marketable qualities, and investments compared with the so-called outputs, namely their salary and professional status. When a person perceives an imbalance between their efforts and their compensation relative to that of others whom they view as similar to themselves, they feel dissatisfied. Their dissatisfactions can be with their salary, their perceived stature compared with similar others, and also the amount of loans they accrued in order to work in the field of their choosing. To illustrate, let's say you take out $100,000 in loans to pay and end up with an annual salary of $75,000. By comparison, another person whom you view as similar to you takes out $50,000 in loans and ends up with an annual salary of $70,000. Equity theory posits that you will be dissatisfied because of a perceived inequality in the ratio of your inputs to outputs versus the other person's ostensibly better ratio of inputs to outputs. Conversely, that other person is likely to feel pretty swell about the situation.

Indeed, several psychologists in my study described what amounted to upward social comparisons with far-better paid and (in their view) more-respected psychiatrists. Considering psychology doctoral students' comparable academic and training requirements in terms of time and money, it is, therefore, not surprising that several participants found the wide disparities in pay between psychologists and psychiatrists difficult to fathom and hard to accept. On the other hand, the much smaller disparity between the participants' compensation as psychologists and that of mental health professionals without doctoral degrees added to their discontent, perceptions of inequity, and diminished sense of professional worth. For example, participant #6 found the fact that psychiatrists at her current job make three times her salary, whereas she makes approximately $5,000 more than Master's-level clinicians, to be "a joke." Participant #7 concurred, noting, "I've worked really hard to get a Ph.D . . . and the fact that [during her postdoctoral year] I was making less money than people with bachelor's degrees,

I felt bitter, I felt resentful and also unappreciated, that people didn't value psychologists, or you know psychology in general, what we can offer to people."

The psychologists also associated repaying loans with a multitude of limitations and sacrifices in their personal lives, as well as difficulties in their social lives. Participant #5 stated, "This is like my little kid; don't think that because you're gonna date a psychologist there's going to be weekend trips to Cancun. I have loans, lots and lots of loans . . . It felt almost like the skeleton in my closet." More generally, the psychologists detailed a sense of delayed or slowed adult development. Participant #1, the oldest person in my study, described, "a sense where you're kind of kept in an adolescent state a lot longer, you know it's like you're never quite grown up, so there's a sense of not being accomplished."

For many, serious debt meant a diminished ability or complete inability to save and invest money for their future, to save enough for a down payment to purchase a house, or even to be able to start a family of their own. Participant #6 remarked, "[My life] still feels like I'm in college to a certain extent where I'm not saving for my future. I mean I am a little but not to the extent that I would like and I really have to watch my budget. My husband and I would like to start a family, but that's been delayed." Some also noted that loan repayment and its overall effect upon their finances reduced both their free time and available money for activities with friends. Others lamented an inability to afford travel costs to visit family located in other parts of the country. In each case, the participants described their loan repayment as problematic and complicating for their most important relationships.

Professional limitations included being unable and/or unwilling to work with lower socioeconomic clientele, as well as an inability to fulfill ethics code standards emphasizing that psychologists should set aside time for pro-bono—free and voluntary—endeavors (American Psychological Association, 2002). In a profession in which the "goodness of fit" is essential between a provider and patient, some of the participating psychologists were unable to find or pursue financially viable work with populations and in clinical settings for which they had the greatest passion and training. Instead, they described taking better-paying positions for which they felt sub-optimally qualified and less enthused, rather than lesser-paying jobs in their areas of expertise. Their trade-off, while better for them financially, carried with it costs to them in the form of ambivalence, guilt, and less job satisfaction. Participant #8 summed up her experience: "I know that my heart lies with a teaching job, that's what I really want to be doing but I know that I can't make the loan payment on that salary. I'm not following my passion, and that's not something I ever thought I would give up."

Related to the personal and professional sacrifices associated with loan repayment, the psychologists in my study also detailed ambivalent experiences of both satisfaction and dissatisfaction about their chosen profession and clinical work in and of itself. Most were content with their work but displeased with its price tag and its payoff, which in turn threatened their contentment. Nevertheless, participant #9 reflected a measured view of her loans relative to her satisfaction as a psychologist. She noted, "I'm doing what I was called to do, and because I made some unwise financial decisions does not mean that somehow my decision to become a psychologist was wrong."

Themes from the third category indicated that the participating psychologists' actual experience of educational debt accrual and repayment was incongruent with their previously held expectations. Several noted having chosen a doctoral degree in psychology because they anticipated a strong financial yield after graduation, but instead they encountered a different, less-fortuitous outcome. Participant #6 stated, "I thought once I graduated I could breathe a sigh of relief, [because] when you say you're a doctor people automatically think you make so much money, and you drive around in a Lexus, and it's, no, I'm driving around in a Honda Civic, because the perception of how much a doctor should make doesn't seem to fit."

In general, the psychologists in my study delayed gratification indefinitely for many of their material desires, and in some cases they experienced difficulties affording monthly bills even for some of life's basic necessities and maintenance. When viewing the degree specifically as a financial investment, several participants expressed doubts about the wisdom and economic utility—also known as its "bottom-line yield"—of pursuing an expensive doctoral degree in psychology.

Participant #7 recalled working in her first position after graduation: "I remember many times coming into work and even my boss asking me, 'Is something bothering you?' and I'd say, 'It's financial stress' and not just the stress itself but the whole idea of, 'This is what I'm getting paid after all I've done.'"

Many of the participating psychologists expressed frustration about their lack of financial education and varying degrees of ignorance about money and debt prior to taking educational loans. Accordingly, several expressed a desire to have had greater guidance and mentorship when making their decisions about their educational loans. They firmly believed that they would have benefited during graduate school from coursework about financing a private practice and/or running a small business. Participant #7 was adamant: "We should have some kind of class on business and how to run a practice, and what happens with managed care and insurance and what does it all mean. We definitely need that, and it's the one place where I feel like the education failed me."

In the fourth category, the participating psychologists described a process of evolving perceptions about their debt accrual and repayment. That is to say, they came to view the repayment of their loans from a broadened perspective with a longer time horizon regarding repayment and its consequences. They indicated that this "longer view" fostered in them an improved capacity to tolerate and come to terms with aspects of repayment they perceived negatively and experienced as burdensome. Additionally, they described experiencing processes of personal growth, which I defined in my study as "the ongoing and increasing acquisition of self-knowledge, self-acceptance, personal confidence, feelings of empowerment, and personal efficacy as an individual." Participant #2 remarked, "This is certainly a hard way of learning [those lessons], but I've gotten a gift from it. I am so much more empowered, and more and more I've found my voice throughout this because there's such a stigma around women and finances."

Several of the psychologists in my study indicated that acclimating to their loan repayment yielded substantial shifts in their values and beliefs about self-promotion, money, its priority in their lives, and thus the value given (or not) to their material acquisitions and aspirations. Most prominently, these psychologists reported increased motivation and activity geared toward learning how to market and self-promote professionally, and increased comfort with charging higher hourly rates and/or negotiating for salary increases. To wit, participant #9 referred to her repayment experience as "a process having had a couple of ebbs, and now we're in a flow." She reflected about her process and perceived three distinct phases/approaches to repayment: "Inactive, reactive, and proactive."

In conclusion, the results of my study suggest ways in which a lack of money, forethought, and/or chronic financial concerns (relative or otherwise) can hinder your ability to fulfill your highest potentials. Equally, the results of my study suggest that money and material wealth, when handled responsibly and with maturity, can provide a stabilizing influence to enable you to meet your most basic needs, and also free you to pursue and attain your goal of becoming a successful and profitable psychologist. In deciding how to finance your education, you would be wise to heed the advice of participant #5, who believed it vital that you "look deep before you leap."

Student Loan Repayment: The Options

Before continuing the discussion on student loan repayment, it is essential to examine the options available to those who are contemplating loans for graduate school in psychology, and/or struggling financially upon graduation. For starters, you should always seek first to obtain *subsidized* federal loans for your education if at all possible. When you take subsidized federal loans, the lender (via the federal government) covers any interest that accumulates while you are in school, or later, in period of agreed-on non-payment. However, due to the credit crisis of 2008–2009, banks and other financial institutions are now placing stricter restrictions on students when they apply for student loans. For instance, banks are requiring credit checks, lines of credit, and other requirements for students—requirements that never existed prior to 2008.

Indeed, changes in lending practices over the past few years have made it more difficult to obtain fully subsidized federal loans, the most common of which are called Stafford loans. Stafford loans are fixed-rate student loans, and typically have a relatively low fixed rate; as of 2012–2013, they have a fixed rate as low as 3.4 percent. Unfortunately, as of July 2012, graduate students are no longer eligible for subsidized Stafford loans. Whereas in the past that 3.4 percent would be taken up by the government while you complete graduate school, now that 3.4 percent will continue to be your responsibility, even while you are completing your graduate studies.

Fortunately, another type of federal loan called Perkins loans continues to be available as a subsidized loan option for many graduate students. In addition to their subsidized status, another advantage of taking Perkins loans is they can qualify for loan forgiveness if you work in a qualifying capacity with underserved populations. This is particularly true if your job includes working with children and families from inner city or rural communities. A downside to Perkins loans is that they are available in smaller, capped quantities than Stafford loans. Subsidized, private, non-federal loans are virtually unheard of, plus private loans tend to come with higher interest rates and more stringent repayment terms.

After graduation, you can count on what's called a *grace period* of roughly six months, at which point you will be expected to begin repaying your loans. However, that may not prove enough time to get your budget in line to afford a sizable monthly payment. In addition, you may have other bills left over from graduate school with higher interest rates, such as credit cards. I strongly recommend first paying off or paying down debts with the least flexibility for repayment and highest interest rates, of which credit cards are paramount. I also believe it is important to develop at least a small nest egg of savings alongside and/ or prior to the onset of beginning your loan repayment. I can personally attest that saving, say, ten grand to have in the bank can make a big difference when you start repaying your loans. That ten grand can help you in a pinch, while also providing a degree of stress relief. Just knowing it's there in the first place is helpful, and it also can be used and replenished in reasonable doses for self-care and to add to your quality of life.

Indeed, failing to save and retain a modest nest egg while moving full steam ahead into your loan repayment can yield heightened financial strain. As you just finished reading, making large loan payments while living paycheck to paycheck without sufficient underlying financial security can be a most unpleasant experience for new psychologists. Nevertheless, don't delude yourself into making lavish expenditures in the name of "self-care" or "quality of life" additions. As before, when you are getting licensed and starting a private practice, you can expect for a time to be a doctor of ramen noodles (I use the phrase loosely). In other words, you should prepare yourself to choose prudence over opulence. Yes, that 2003 Honda Civic with 150,000 miles and 40 miles per gallon runs just fine in the near-term. Don't even look at the Mercedes-Benz of U.S.A. website. You can check out that website five years down the road after you've read this book, worked hard, and become financially successful.

In order to obtain more breathing room, you can request a *deferment* or *forbearance* on your repayment. The term "loan deferment" means explaining to your lender that you would like some extra time to begin paying off your student loans after your grace period has ended. The term "forbearance" means requesting to have your payments reduced or suspended for a period of time. Either may be a good, short-term option during the lean months of preparing for licensure in psychology, starting a practice, and/or building that nest egg. Often times, if you qualify, you are allotted loan deferment for up to a three-year period, and even longer for forbearances. In fact, your financial institution is sometimes required to offer mandatory forbearance.

During a period of forbearance, interest invariably continues to accrue, which is one reason why obtaining a forbearance from lenders tends to be easier than obtaining deferment. It's also related to why longer periods of forbearance are granted at the outset of repayment— lenders can be assured of interest continuing to accumulate during forbearance, which is not always the case during periods of deferment. If you have subsidized loans and are granted a deferment on the basis of unemployment or economic hardship, then you are provided with what amounts to another grace period. You will not be required to make monthly payments, and interest will not be *capitalizing* during the deferment.

To speak of capitalization is to speak of a process in which the interest on your loans is added to the principal, or original sum total, of your loans every few months. Typically, capitalization occurs in quarterly increments throughout the year. Capitalization may sound like no big deal, and initially it's merely the sum total of interest. However, there's a catch. If you don't pay off the interest as it accumulates, the interest will begin to accumulate on the principal *plus* the interest that already has accumulated. Another way to describe this is the interest *compounds* upon itself. So if you start out with $100,000 to pay back, let's say $4,500 in interest is added in year one, to make a total of $104,500 owed. Over the next year, the interest that capitalizes is likely to be more in the neighborhood of $5,000, because it will be capitalizing on the compounded sum of $104,500 rather than the original $100,000. And so on and so forth, with bigger financial implications the higher up the student loan ladder you go.

Thus, you should be careful about choosing deferment or forbearance, because delaying the inevitable often is not free, and can be costly. To repeat: delaying the inevitable often is not free, and can be costly. You do not want to live in a false, utopian world in which you are not paying your debts while the total to be repaid quietly turns into that elephant in the waiting room. In addition to the above-noted practical and calculable considerations, starting loan repayment sooner rather than later also is a psychologically sound decision. In addition to forcing yourself to be realistic about the contours of your financial life, you also guard against becoming stuck in a position of passivity and/or reactivity, a key component of perceived financial strain.

Sometimes, you may not be able to afford your entire payment, but paying something at all can be better than nothing. Or as a favorite saying of mine goes, "The perfect is the enemy of the good." For example, depending on your financial situation, you may want to consider forbearance while continuing to make interest payments. This is almost always allowed by lenders, and may make some sense when you are starting a private practice, especially if your interest payments aren't prohibitive. Ultimately, paying something towards your loans to keep the interest from becoming a runaway train is something you will be able to feel good about in the short term and can be of great value to you in the long run.

Conversely, holding off indefinitely on any form of repayment, especially if done without a plan of action for your eventual repayment, requires a form of passive mental effort to block out the looming reality of repayment from your daily consciousness. Delaying any repayment can foster distress as you begin your career and/or begin to build your private practice. By contrast, beginning repayment sooner rather than later moves you psychologically into a position of proactive engagement, which can be an empowering experience that dampens rather than feeds financial stress and anxiety. It can free up your energies to focus more effectively on your clinical work and the development of your practice. In other words, as participant #9 alluded, it is best to move from a position of inactivity/reactivity to a position of proactivity as swiftly as possible.

In general, you should not defer loan repayment for the full three years continuously unless it is absolutely necessary. Let's examine a final scenario to illustrate the point. Consider if you do a one-year deferment on a $150,000 loan at 5 percent. This means that you will add $7,500 as an interest payment. Yet, if you have a three-consecutive-year deferment, that $7,500 jumps to $22,500, and actually even higher when accounting for compounding interest. That's an increase of no less than $15,000. Trust me, when you are starting a private practice in clinical psychology, making up $15,000 takes a good deal of time and effort. Not counting taxes, that's essentially 15 psychological evaluations that you need to complete at $1,000 apiece. And many psychological evaluations do not pay $1,000, so if you are doing them for $500 each, now you're up to 30 just to get back to even.

Another point to consider is that once the total months allotted for deferment and forbearance are over, you will be at your lender's mercy to graciously offer additional time for deferments or forbearance. Should any life emergencies occur requiring you to pause repayment, lacking leverage vis-à-vis your lender is unlikely to be helpful. I think you understand here that there are major personal and financial considerations when it comes to student loan deferment or forbearance.

If you decide that you do not want to do student loan deferment or forbearance, it may be possible for you to change your payment plan, depending on your loan officer and the financial institution. One form of repayment that can be particularly helpful is called *income-based repayment*, which is exactly as it sounds. If you are able to qualify for this form of repayment, the amount you owe in any given month will directly correspond with your income level. If your income goes up, your payments will go up as a proportion of the increase. Likewise, should your income decrease for any reason, so too will your required monthly payment. Yet here again, you must work with you lender first to determine if you qualify for income-based repayment. Second, you should be careful not to willy-nilly switch over to income-based repayment, especially if involves a longer term of repayment. Payments proportionate to your income can alleviate some of the financial strain of repayment, but the interest that accumulates is not based upon your income, and is always based upon the sum total of your loans. Therefore, if income-based repayment stretches out your repayment by many years, the tradeoff over time may be substantially greater amounts of compounding interest and much more money to pay back overall.

Another option is debt *consolidation*, which means that you are merging your loans. Typically, federal loans offer the lowest interest rates and do not sell your loans to the highest bidder, as banks often do. Again, this is not a surprising practice, since banks are financial institutions designed to make money. If you choose debt consolidation, a website that APA notes can help you is https://www.myedaccount. com/, which assists you with consolidating your loans (http://www. apa.org/gradpsych/2010/09/cover-fear.aspx). Consolidation in and of itself also merges your interest rates into a single interest rate, which may or may not be helpful to you. For example, if you have $125,000 in loans at 4 percent interest, and another $25,000 at 8 percent interest, and the consolidation offers you a 5.75 percent interest rate on the full $150,000, it is not likely a good idea to consolidate. You'll be better off paying down the loans separately than accepting a substantially higher interest rate on 5/6th of your loans.

Indeed, there are concerns with debt consolidation as a practice, especially for those of you with substantial loans from private lenders. For instance, eminent financial expert Dave Ramsey warns against debt consolidation. He notes that debt consolidation is simply moving debt and not changing debt (http://www.daveramsey.com/article/the-truth-about-debt-consolidation/). He summarizes this very good point—a contention that accords with the overall theme of Dr. Bargreen's book: "Debt consolidation seems appealing because there is a lower interest rate on some of the debt and a lower payment. However, in almost every case we review, we find that the lower payment exists not because the rate is actually lower but because the term is extended. If you stay in debt longer, you get a lower payment, but if you stay in debt longer, you pay the lender more, which is why they are in the debt consolidation business . . . they make money off of you" (http://www. daveramsey.com/article/the-truth-about-debt-consolidation/).

Ramsey makes good sense, because the idea is to pay off your loans, not to just lower your payments, which means that it will take longer to pay them off. These are also institutions designed to make a profit. Once you do the math, you can see that in many cases, just lowering your payment can hinder you financially. You want to gain financial freedom, not to extend your lack of financial freedom. Another concern with extending your debt is that it may be more difficult for you to apply for other loans, such as mortgages and car loans, if the bank sees that you have extended yourself for many years on your student loans. Bottom line: unless you are making major improvements to your interest rates and monthly repayment options, and/or unless you are fully committed to exceeding the repayment terms by paying off your debt more aggressively in the future when money isn't as tight, it is best to pay off your student loans as quickly as possible.

One final option to consider pursuing is *loan forgiveness*, which typically entails a government program (municipal, state, federal, and military). Should you qualify, in exchange for fulfilling a period of work to a targeted community or population, one of the above-noted institutions will agree to eventually wipe the slate clean for the remainder of your loans. A pamphlet entitled "Psychologist Participation in Student Loan Repayment" (Hawley, 2007) can serve as a guide to available options for student loan repayment. Available opportunities include faculty loan repayment programs, National Institute of Health (NIH) repayment programs, Department of Veteran Affairs programs, serving as a psychologist in the reserve forces of one of branches of the United States military, and National Health Service Corps programs.

These programs may be viable options for those not wanting to start their private practice right away. However, it is important to note, as

Dr. Bargreen explains convincingly, that based on income potential alone, developing a profitable private practice is perhaps the most logical and economical option that will enable you to pay off your loans most quickly. Furthermore, loan-forgiveness programs typically are difficult to obtain and may require you to relocate to less-desirable areas than your current locale. In the case of the armed forces reserves, they are unable to offer guarantees that you will not be called up to active duty. Furthermore, many of these programs require you to have completed a full-time internship accredited by the American Psychological Association. If you've taken another route, you're flatly out of luck.

Others programs are less prohibitive, such as public service loan forgiveness. However, even here they require employment in the public sector, which can be difficult to obtain at a time where many state governments have instituted hiring and pay freezes. Public service loan forgiveness, as I can personally attest through my full-time capacity working in a New York state psychiatric hospital, requires a full decade of employment without being delinquent on any payments throughout that time period. They also require loan consolidation through a federal program called Direct Loan Consolidation; thus, if you leave the public sector before making 120 payments, you'll have consolidated your loans without loan forgiveness. As noted earlier, if you are not careful, loan consolidation can be costly over time. Lastly, the public service loan forgiveness plan is unable to guarantee actual forgiveness of your debts until 2017 for the first cohort, given that the program began in 2007. Even then, considering the already gargantuan and growing national debt, there are no guarantees the federal government will be able to follow through on public service forgiveness. In fact, being part of public service loan forgiveness does not in fact guarantee you loan forgiveness after 10 years, but rather guarantees the opportunity to apply for and advocate for said forgiveness.

A final option to consider is working in a correctional facility. In exchange for the oft strenuous and at times dangerous demands of the work, the pay for prison work tends to be better and loan forgiveness options can be plentiful. Not surprisingly, however, there tends to be a high dropout rate, as some have compared working in a prison to working in a dungeon. Others, including those capable of acclimating to working in a penitentiary environment, still tend to encounter many uniquely challenging moral, ethical, and psychological difficulties from working with incarcerated populations.

For example, Dr. Bargreen recently described to me his impressions from a trip he made to a correctional facility while in graduate school in California. He found the staff psychologists to be a "different breed" of psychologist. He keenly remembered that the staff had a somewhat glazed-over detached demeanor, with an apparently limited range of emotionality. It stands to reason that cultivating a degree of aloofness and desensitization is not only necessary but is also vital for coping with the psychological taxing and challenging work. Make no mistake: doing so can change you as a person, not only professionally but also personally. I also know of several colleagues who took jobs in prisons. One described to me his experiences running group therapy programming with patients confined to individual cages in the room. He met with others individually while in shackles, and all the while he was mindful of the ever-present potential for violence and riots. Not exactly a cheery business; at least it would seem so to those of us on the outside looking in.

Nevertheless, some prisons not only pay six-figure annual salaries, they also offer generous benefits packages and loan-forgiveness program, and can be a great way to knock out your student loans and accumulate savings. That said, I would be wary of seeking work in a prison unless you first accumulate a good deal of experience working with the courts, jails, sex offenders, and/or other difficult populations. In psychology, it is essential to "know thyself," and this is especially important when contemplating whether the rewards are worth the risks inherent in the starkly forensic environment of prisons.

In sum, although loan-forgiveness programs may work and be of great benefit to some, they are not easily obtainable and have many strings attached. Clearly, with so many uncertainties, both in qualifying for a loan-forgiveness program and in what is required to ensure that you receive loan forgiveness, they should not be taken for granted in your plans for loan repayment. Given this, if your goal is to be in business for yourself and to be as profitable and free of student loan debt as quickly as possible, it makes the most sense to build your practice and begin to pay down your loans as soon as possible after graduate school. If you delay the process of loan repayment, you're just delaying the inevitable.

References

American Psychological Association. (2002). Ethical principles of psychologists and code of conduct. *American Psychologist, 57*(12), 1060-1073.

Baum, S., & O'Malley, M. (2003). *College on credit: how borrowers perceive their educational debt; Results of the 2002 national student loan survey.* Braintree, MA: Nellie Mae Corporation.

Beggs, J. M. (2002). Income, subjective well-being and the comparative perspective: an examination of relative income and its possible comparison standards. Ph.D. dissertation, Saint Louis University, Missouri. Retrieved from ProQuest Digital Dissertations database (Publication No. AAT3051776)

Dolgan, J. (2004). *Contractual therapeutic involvement.* Unpublished doctoral paper, Graduate School of Professional Psychology, University of Denver.

Graham, S. (February 2008). It's time to do something about our future. *Independent Practitioner, 28*(1), 10.

Hawley, G. (2007) Psychologist Participation in Student Loan Repayment. Presented at APA Annual Convention, August 19, 2007. Retrieved from www.apa.org/careers/early-career/loan-replayment.pdf

Wicherski, M., & Kohout, J. (2007). 2005 doctorate employment survey. Washington, DC: American Psychological Association.

4

GRADUATE SCHOOL

Master's Programs

This may be a good option if you feel that you can't get into a doctoral program. Think about the Master's programs that will make it possible for you to be accepted into a doctoral program in the future. There are some advantages and disadvantages of going this route. One major disadvantage is that many doctoral programs do not accept credits from a Master's program. Some do but many don't, which means that you will have to spend more money, unless your master's program is paid for. If your Master's program is not paid for, you will essentially be paying for two more years of school, which goes against one of my main premises that you want to complete graduate school as quickly as possible in order to save money. Stopping your education at the Master's level in psychology is not worthwhile, as reimbursement rates for Master's-level clinicians are typically poor. There is also a surplus of Master's-level clinicians throughout the country, which means that it is difficult to get a job once you have completed your program. Many of the jobs that Master's-level clinicians take end up leaving the persons overworked and underpaid. Please, do not take this route if you are able to get into a doctoral program. I promise that you will thank me someday. Also, remember you complete your Master's degree partway through many doctoral programs.

The Master's programs also can be very expensive. An in-state program might run you $5K–$10K per year, while an out-of-state program can be $20K or more per year. That is a huge expense, on top of another five-plus years for a doctoral program. If you have student loans for the Master's program, this is going to mean that you will need more time to pay off your debt once you are in practice some-day. The financial burden of starting through a Master's program can be very heavy. This is why I would not recommend that you go this route, unless you are set on applying to one of the top doctoral pro-grams, as some of them require that you have a Master's degree in psychology (or related field). Doing the math, we can explore more how a Master's degree might be a financial burden. Master's degrees in psychology take two years. Let's say that you have $40K of student loans out of the two years. But tacking on 5 percent interest on the loans is $42K. That means you start out $42K in the hole. Assuming that you start a doctoral program right after the Master's program and that it takes you five years to complete the doctoral program, that puts your Master's degree debt at $47K. Adding $80K of doctoral degree debt at 5 percent interest for five years takes the total amount of debt to $131K, instead of $84K for the doctoral program. You are talking about paying 64 percent more than you need to here! That is just a ton of money. Think about how much longer it will take to pay off $131K instead of $84K. It might take an extra 10 years to pay off that dif-ference! Plus, you will be accruing 5 percent interest during that time, which will make those figures even more polarizing.

Now to the advantages. One major advantage of being in a Master's program is that when you come to the doctoral-level work, you will have experience taking some of the same classes and your knowledge base in psychology will likely eclipse that of your peers. While the Master's program could give you more experience learning about top-ics in psychology, I'm not sure that is the best argument for being in a Master's program, since you should receive a broad spectrum of learning in a doctoral program. But taking more classes in psychology should make life for you easier in the doctoral program, particularly if you were not a psychology major and did not take many psychol-ogy courses in your undergrad program. A Master's program will also help you to learn more about your likes and dislikes in psychology, which will likely make it easier for you to choose your dissertation topic—and, hopefully, will make completing a dissertation easier. Going through a Master's program will also likely make you more familiar with both research and clinical work, as you will likely have some more experience in those realms. So, as you can see, there are some advantages and disadvantages to completing a Master's program before a doctoral program. In general, I would advise against applying to a Master's program unless you want to get into an elite doctoral program, such as Stanford or Yale.

Doctoral Programs

Grad school is nothing short of an exhausting process. If you have been accepted into a doctoral program in clinical psychology, congratulations. Now be prepared to work hard. For some, the process will be less arduous. For others, this will be a total disaster if you don't push yourself to the limit. Each program is going to be different. My program was largely clinically based, so I had a heavy dose of classes, tests, and comprehensive exams (comps). The comps are tests that attempt to prove your proficiency in specific domains of psychology, such as statistics, physiological psychology, or personality theory. Some of the comps were tough and some were so difficult that people didn't pass them . . . ever. I was fortunate to pass the Biological Basis of Behavior Comp—an exam that closely resembled a crap shoot. You throw your dice out there and hope that it lands on red. The first time I took it, I landed on black. A crushing blow.

Most doctoral programs in clinical psychology have core classes that you will need to take as part of being an APA-approved program. While most people in graduate school for psychology will have a good background on some of the course material, I was surprised to find how in-depth the grad school courses were compared to the classes that I had taken during my undergraduate years. Generally, graduate school classes include courses in statistics, tests and measurements, experimental psychology, psychopathology, personality theory, psychotherapy techniques, and multicultural psychology, as well as dissertation classes, clinical supervision classes, community psychology, history of psychology, and, in some cases, industrial/organizational psychology classes. Many programs have classes required for psychological testing—classes such as cognitive assessment, objective personality assessment, projective personality assessment, and a clinical inference class, which is a capstone course for psychological report writing. As I have indicated previously, it is imperative that you take courses in psychological testing, because otherwise you will be taking away roughly half of your earning potential as a psychologist. Because being a financially successful psychologist means doing psychological testing, and regularly, you need to find a program that is strong in psychological testing. There may be some programs that only offer a few courses in psychological testing. I would not apply to these programs. I feel that if they are a program that only specializes in training psychotherapists, then they are only offering half of what a psychologist does.

Each clinical program requires a doctoral student to take clinical supervision classes. The clinical supervision classes are particularly valuable opportunities to consult with colleagues and clinical psychologists about difficult cases. There are a variety of options here. Some of the classes are based on psychodynamic, humanistic, or a variety of therapeutic orientations. Some also will be based on psychologically testing. This is an opportunity to learn more about applying theory to practice. At the point that you take the clinical supervision class, you will be well acquainted with the various personality theories. If you are interested in behavioral theory, choose an instructor who promotes this orientation. I strongly encourage you to choose a clinical supervision instructor who is experienced in psychological testing. Otherwise, you will be only gaining supervision in psychotherapy. Try to find a clinical supervision instructor who is a strong therapist and evaluator.

I was in a clinical supervision class with the same instructor for two years. After some research I found Dr. Tobias, a clinical supervisor who had a wealth of psychological testing and forensic psychology experience. Dr. Tobias was trained in psychoanalytic theory, which also appealed to me. His case conceptualizations were fascinating and were well connected to a clinical practice that I saw myself having someday. Dr. Tobias was particularly adept at asking good questions of students who were presenting on clinical cases. His feedback was exceptional. I thought this class was so good that I had another good friend join the group. My friend was disillusioned with his previous clinical supervision instructor, who was rude and pompous. My friend's instructor was so rude that he told my friend that he was dressing like a five-year-old.

Talk about inappropriate! So choose your clinical supervision instructor wisely. You might learn just as much as you do from your internship site instructors. I learned so much from mine that I wanted him to be a reader for my dissertation. Dr. Tobias was a great asset for my dissertation, as he was very well versed with psychological testing and the MMPI-2. You definitely want people in your corner when it comes to the dissertation. Take the clinical supervision class very seriously. It is very likely that you will learn almost as much from the class as you do from your internship sites.

Again, do your own research into the clinical supervision instructors and also make sure to talk to your colleagues about what they have heard about specific clinical supervision class instructors, just as it is important to ask about the clinical supervisors at the internship sites. Some programs also require a supervision course and a certain amount of elective classes, as well. The supervision course is where you supervise first- or second-year grad students. This is not an easy class, but it teaches you about the supervisory process and leadership style. Typically, a doctoral program requires taking four or five years of coursework, depending on how many classes you can fit in. Some of these classes are going to be more difficult and will have more requirements than others. Consider talking to students who have taken the classes before if you have concerns about a certain class. I found that it was particularly helpful to learn about the professors from the students. Students also will be able to inform you about the professors' teaching styles and you can use that information to your advantage. For instance, if you are good at retaining lectures, you will not struggle with a professor that lectures for hours. But other students struggle with retaining what they hear in lectures, and learn better with information presented to them visually. Some professors will employ a more visual style of teaching. And your learning style is important to consider when learning about the different professors and their teaching styles.

Graduate school will require you to have two- to-three-year-long clinical internships. Sometimes these begin in the first year, and some are in the second year, as usually each program has a "practicum" that prepares you for a full internship. The practicum is usually fewer hours than the internship and will afford you valuable clinical experience. If your school does not have a practicum program, I strongly recommend that you do something clinically related during the summer. The practicum is similar to going to the minor leagues before you make it to the majors. I will talk more about clinical internships later, but make sure to choose internships that are in an area of psychology that interests you. Consider challenging yourself with these—do not just accept an internship because you have heard from other students that it is an easy one. Talk to other students and get a variety of opinions on the internship site.

I would strongly consider finding a program that includes a practicum, as well as two internships. The extra year that you gain from the practicum will likely benefit you as a clinical psychologist someday. In my practicum, I was able to become familiar with psychometrics and psychological tests that I did not learn in my assessment class. I learned about memory tests, such as the Wechsler Memory Scales, and the Rey Complex Figure test, and my supervisor had more than 30 years of experience using the instruments. Learning these memory tests has been invaluable, as I regularly do memory assessments in my clinical practice. Memory testing is another way that psychologists can be financially successful and can differentiate themselves from other professions.

I found that some of the more difficult classes that had the most requirements were personality theory classes, such as psychodynamic theory, behavioral theory, and humanistic theory. These classes require a great deal of reading, and exams in these domains tended to be very comprehensive. The theory classes were particularly difficult for me because I had not taken the theory courses in my undergraduate studies, so they were generally foreign ideas. Some people find learning behavioral theory a cakewalk, while I struggled with some of the concepts. It took time for me to make sense with ideas like operant conditioning and reinforcements.

Other classes that I found demanding were the psychotherapy technique classes, such as humanistic techniques and group therapy techniques. While these classes were difficult, I also found them to be the most fascinating and also the most applicable to the clinical work that I do now. The demands of each class will vary from program to program. However, I have heard similar contentions from my colleagues in both Washington and southern California.

Many colleagues complain to me that they struggled to find inspiration while they were in graduate school. It is possible that they just didn't find the right instructors, but I think that they might have been either looking in the wrong places or it is possible that they didn't look hard enough. I think that it is essential to find individual faculty members who are inspiring. I think that when you lack inspiration, you have a tendency to move toward stagnation. And you don't want to be stagnant at any point during the doctoral program. There will be highs and lows and not every professor will inspire you, but you want to find inspiration. This is all part of the process of finishing your program quickly. When you finish quickly, you save money and will be more financially successful. It is worth noting that what one finds inspiring depends on the individual and individual interests in psychology. For me, there were a few incredibly inspirational instructors who stood out.

Dr. Joanne Callan, a psychoanalyst who interviewed me at my graduate school, was one of those special professors. Dr. Callan had incredible poise and confidence. Teaching seemed effortless to her and she always did such a good job with questions and content. Some of the articles that we read in Psychodynamic Theory class were complicated and advanced for a first-year student. But she helped make sense of the content and made learning psychodynamic theory fun. I'm a bit biased because I find Freud and his contemporaries to be particularly fascinating, not only from a theory standpoint but also from a historical perspective. I mean, Freud is probably the first person to ever create a complex psychological theory. I took as many classes from Dr. Callan as possible.

Another inspiring professor was Dr. Jose Lichtszajn. Dr. Lichtszajn was half-Mexican and half-Polish. Addressing the class in a strong Hispanic accent, he was empowering to students, told hilarious jokes, and was always engaging. He was the perfect person to teach my Intro to Psychotherapy class, because he had so many facets of the integral theories of psychology memorized. The man was a walking dictionary. When he was lecturing, he was one of those people who seemed like they knew everything about everything. Because he had been in the field so long, he had many intriguing case studies and anecdotes about his private practice. He had the perfect marriage of teaching theory and applying that to case studies from his private practice. His tests were unbearably complex and difficult. But you respected the man for making them so complicated and he respected us for memorizing as much as was humanly possible. Having such a wealth of clinical experience, Dr. Lichtszajn was one of those people who was an unreal clinician but a better human being. I took as many classes from Dr. Lichtszajn as possible. He came to my graduation dinner and it was an honor to have him there. My point here is that you need to look for your inspiration from the faculty of your program. And keep on learning from those who inspire you. This will help you push forward and put that Dr. Smith diploma on your wall.

But don't only look to professors for inspiration. Graduate school can be a time when you can learn a great deal about yourself and what truly interests you. Maybe you become interested in surfing or yoga. Maybe you find your passion in food and wine. You might begin your passion for the arts, the symphony, or musicals. Follow your fascination in your free time. Not that you will have a ton of free time, but to be successful in graduate school, it is essential that you find passionate non-academic subjects that you integrate to cope with the grind of your everyday graduate school life. And please, make sure that these interests are productive and helpful. Smoking pot every day is not a productive or helpful passion. Building houses with the United Way or mountain hiking are productive and helpful passions.

For me, I became more passionate about food and wine. One thing that I found so amazing about food and wine is the diversity of both subjects. I find it incredible that pinot noir can be grown in Oregon, New Zealand, France, and Chile. I similarly find it amazing that American BBQ can differ by city. And each is excellent in its own right. I acquired a bunch of hobbies while I was in graduate school. I learned more about mountain hiking and chose to cope with my school stress by weight lifting on a near-daily basis. Weight-lifting was empowering and also was a great way to relieve stress. There are few stress relievers better than blazing a trail across Mt. Whitney. My fellow student, Danny, and I would do long day-hikes on Mt. Whitney every few months. We would leave at 6AM and return at 8PM. Those were great and incredibly uplifting days. These were some of the ways that I coped with the mentally taxing and strenuous schedule for five years. I think that for you to finish grad school quickly, it is essential to find and integrate your passions into your lifestyle while you are in your doctoral program.

If you have moved away from your family, I recommend trying to visit your friends and family regularly. You will make friends once you begin grad school but it is likely that most of your support group, especially when you begin grad school, will reside in the area where you have been living. Go back to visit them and to maintain those relationships. Especially when you first begin grad school, it is important to feel supported. Some programs offer a summer or some summers off. If you have any time off during your first or second years, I strongly recommend taking a trip. This doesn't have to be a lavish trip around the world. But this can be a trip back home for a week, a visit to Disneyland, or something like that. The trip will help with your work/life balance. It will also give you something to look forward to, especially since you will likely be planning it well in advance. I decided to take a road trip during my second year of grad school and that served as a great way to really see most of the state of California. It was a great break from my class work and practicum and wasn't very expensive. You will likely be living your life on a budget, so if you are a bargain hunter, find a deal of a reasonably priced trip and go for it. Do it your first or second year, because it is likely that you will become too busy after that.

Grad school will teach you a lot about perseverance. Sometimes, it is going to seem like it will never end. In your first year, you might have a mentor die, as I did. And then subsequently bomb your next exam, as I did. Who knows, maybe you will suffer a more serious trauma, like the death of a parent or spouse. You will go through the trials and tribulations as each grain of sand slowly makes its way down the hourglass. But slowly, after each year passes, you realize that you are getting closer to the prize. Your eyes are getting bigger as you gaze at that mental image of the Dr. Smith diploma hanging from the wall. And just when you think that it is there on your wall, you are hit with the dissertation.

Who completes the dissertation? Want the staggering statistics? You've gotten in? Congrats, because you better work hard. Some U.S. universities have set a 10-year limit for students in PhD programs, or refuse to consider graduate credit older than 10 years as counting toward a PhD degree. Overall, 57 percent of students who begin a PhD program in the United States will complete their degree within 10 years, approximately 30 percent will drop out or will be dismissed, and the remaining 13 percent of students will continue on past 10 years (U.S. Department of Education, 2006).

Remember that you don't want to be in that 43 percent that don't finish grad school. Not meaning to scare you, but it can happen. One thing that I can recommend if you are currently in grad school is to know your strengths and weaknesses. Some people are strong writers and will likely push through the dissertation without major problems. That is like me. Some other people are strong test-takers and will push through the comp exams with little effort. That was not me. Some people are so intelligent and gifted that they will do well on everything they lay a hand on in grad school. That was not me. Look in the mirror . . . that is likely not you, either. In fact, I can only name one of my colleagues from grad school who was that way. A good friend of mine, we called him Princeton, among other nicknames. He also possessed a genius-level IQ and waltzed through all academic realms. Since genius IQ is found in less than .1 percent of the population, that is likely not you.

This next part is fairly obvious. If you are not a gifted writer, you are going to have to work harder on the papers and on the dissertation. Prepare yourself. Read the book on APA style. No, really read it. It will help in the long run. You might also want to consider reading many journal articles that will provide a good template for you. The more you read in APA style, the more familiar you will be with writing in that way. Also, please choose articles that are interesting to you. If they are not interesting, you probably won't read them. Have a colleague edit your papers. Pay them if needed. Go to a writing center if you are really struggling. Take the feedback from the professors seriously. Do not blow that off. If they are saying that you need to work on your writing, make it happen . . . work on it. Take the extra steps for success. It will be well worth the headaches.

Prepare early for the dissertation. This means starting before all of your colleagues. The dissertation will likely take longer than expected, with few exceptions. So begin your research and literature review early.

Choose your dissertation chair before others. Work with him or her, and talk about your potential research designs. You may need to join a dissertation class, as many programs have a formal class that you take while you are writing the dissertation. This dissertation group will give you good feedback on your potential ideas and will also be a good support throughout the arduous process. When you are in your first year of graduate school, you should be thinking about potential dissertation topics. Think about what areas interest you. Think about whether you want to do qualitative or quantitative research. What topics are really meaningful to you in psychology? I chose two areas of interest and passion for me: the MMPI-2 and domestic violence. I combined them in choosing my dissertation topic by creating a personality profile for male victims of domestic violence. It was new MMPI-2 research and was a fascinating topic that kept me going through the long (and at times boring) dissertation process.

You will have to take many exams in grad school. If you are not a good test taker, over-prepare for the exams. In this case, you want to prepare for the exams early, so that you can feel confident about the material. I experienced a fair amount of test anxiety. In a doctoral program, you will likely have to complete therapy for yourself as a patient. So if you struggle with test anxiety, talk about it in your sessions. Work through the issues. Get extra help from professors when needed. Ask them for clarification if things do not make sense. And some of the world of psychology simply does not make sense.

Either way, it is good to have an excellent work ethic in grad school. You don't want to be on the wrong end of that 43 percent that don't make it through. You want to be a 57 percenter. So work harder than the next person. That's what I did. That's why I am financially successful right now. I work harder. People are going to recognize your work ethic, too. Professors will notice, colleagues will notice, supervisors will notice. There is really no reason not to work hard. I know . . . it's been a long road . . . lots of classes, lots of lectures, thousands of hours studying for exams, thousands of ethics lectures, thousands of case consultations. The endless hours can be mundane. But think about this. As mundane as the lectures may be, some may be more interesting than others. And for the most part, we have nothing short of an incredibly interesting field. The great thing about psychology is that, clinically speaking, if you want to have a job where you will never be bored, you can find it. You want to never be bored? Spend a year in a psychiatric hospital. That's what I did. I wanted a challenge for my final internship and I sure got one. The psychiatric hospital was near the Mexican border, around 30 minutes from San Diego. The psychological interns did psychological testing and therapy. The incredibly wide spectrum of the DSM IV TR was shown every day. We saw everything from cognitive disorders to dissociative disorders. And plenty of psychopathology, as well. It was certainly never a dull moment under the direction of Dr. Jon Nachison. Dr. Nachison, a psychologist for more than 20 years, guided us through the process, supported us, and helped us learn how to tackle some of the biggest psychological issues out there. It was a great year.

Psych Testing

One of the biggest problems that I have with some programs in clinical psychology is that they do not focus enough on psychological testing. Some people in grad school do not receive proper training on psychological testing. I can see how many people do not enjoy psychological testing. But not offering classes on the Rorschach or not focusing on testing at all is a colossal mistake. Psychological testing is part of the job of being a psychologist. We need to know these things, not only for the licensing exam but because it is truly part of our jobs. It is worth noting that psychology as a profession was largely built out of our ability to test intelligence. Psychology was not built on psychotherapy, it was built on psychological testing. Not learning about psychological testing would be like a mechanic going through mechanic school without learning about how to fix brakes. He would say, "But I know how to fix engines so well and I will never be fixing brakes." The next day, someone comes in with a car needing a brake job and the mechanic is out of luck. He sends him to someone else and just lost a customer. More importantly, he just lost money.

People who are in graduate school do not understand that psychologists do not make real money doing therapy. They make money, that is for sure. But you do not make $100K+ doing therapy all day. OK, you might if you are charging $200 an hour and are seeing five-plus patients per day for private pay. But most people don't do that. And you certainly won't be able to do that just out of grad school. Sorry to burst your bubble like that.

Psychological testing is where the money is in psychology. You need to protect your future, so take classes and internships on psychological testing. That's what I did. And now I am financially successful. Listen, don't only do psychological testing, either, as you want to have breadth of experience in grad school. But don't pigeonhole yourself. Give it a chance, study the books. Learn about the world of Millon, Rorschach, Minnesota Multiphasic Personality Inventory. Read Exner, Greene, Dallstrom, and other eminent writers in psychological testing. It is going to be worth your time in the long run.

Learn about the new tests, because testing corporations are constantly changing their editions of the tests. Know the differences between the WAIS-III and WAIS-IV. You will need to know about the WMS-IV. Do the research and study the tests well. This will pay off in the long run. Make sure to choose internships where you will be using the most relevant and useful, as well as psychometrically sound psychological instruments. If the internship site is still using the WMS-III, you are going to have a problem. While reliability and validity rates are generally similar in both the III and IV, APA clearly states that we need to use the new tests. You don't want to ever be in trouble for using an outdated instrument.

Well, what about when I finish grad school and I have to buy the instruments? How am I going to afford that? Well, the answer is simple; you are going to have to set aside some cash for that. Take a loan out. Trust me, these instruments will pay for themselves . . . many, many times over. For instance, let's say that you do a WAIS-IV and clinical interview. Some government agencies reimburse you about $450 for that. You would only have to do roughly three of these evaluations to pay for the instrument. Given that you will be doing probably 100 of them (hopefully, and really, you should!), you will easily pay for the instrument. You just have to realize that you'll have to buy these things. It is well worth it.

People in grad school have the misconception that they are going to set up shop in Beverly Hills following grad school, charge rich housewives $200 an hour for therapy and live off that. That is not the real world. Now, I am sure that there are psychologists doing that right as I type these words. Good for them, rich housewives need love, too. But, look, you are not going to be seeing that clientele straight out of grad school. You are likely going to be seeing the toxic couple that needs help, the amphetamine-dependent father who needs a psych eval for general assistance, those types. If you don't recognize the real people that you will be seeing, you are living in a fantasy world. And seeing those who are struggling is wonderful and meaningful. Yes, I know it doesn't seem like it right now as you prepare for your comp evaluation. Just wait until you start studying for the EPPP! I don't want to crush your dreams here, I just want you to recognize the likelihood of what your work will be out of grad school. Seeing the world through a realistic lens is a good thing.

Practicum

As stated earlier, some doctoral programs require a practicum in clinical psychology. Some programs, such as UCLA's doctoral program, require a two-year practicum and then a one-year internship. Others, like my program at California School of Professional Psychology, San Diego, required a one-year practicum and two clinical internships. Typically, in the practicum, you are placed in local agencies, such as hospitals, autism centers, private schools, crisis houses, and other community mental health settings. These settings are not always glamorous. For instance, some of the crisis houses in San Diego are mentally taxing and can be unsanitary. I have had many of my colleagues tell me a varied range of experience at crisis houses, and the same can be true for hospital placements. I do not want to discourage you to choose a difficult placement, like a crisis house. But the truth is that as a private practice clinical psychologist you likely will not be doing a great deal of crisis work. Unless you are given the opportunity to perform assessments at the crisis house or psychiatric hospital, I would not choose this as a practicum. I chose a psychiatric hospital for an internship and was given the chance to perform many evaluations, so there was more value with doing both therapy and assessment.

In 2006, the APA required all APA accredited doctoral programs to have a practicum, which would be a one-year supervised experience, prior to having a clinical internship. Most practicums in doctoral programs require fewer hours than internships. This was the case in my program, as my practicum required roughly 10 hours per week. The practicums are typically fewer hours because you are taking a full course load, along with having the practicum. Basically, you should be expected to be busier having a practicum on top of fulltime classes. During this time, you will be extremely busy and will likely not have much of a social life. Practicum hours have been changing as well, as many schools have increased the hour requirements for these programs. For instance, my school increased the number of hours from 800 to 1,000 before I started my practicum.

Similar to the internship, it is essential to carefully choose your supervisor at the practicum site. My supervisor was very experienced in both personality and cognitive assessment. He had been a military psychologist for 30 years and had performed thousands of assessments. Brusque and serious, my practicum supervisor's style of supervision was not for everyone. But it worked for me, as I learned from his wealth of experience. I can't place a value on the amount of cognitive and personality assessments that I performed that year. My experience at my first practicum site is a large reason why I do so many assessments in my clinical practice today.

You might consider doing an obscure practicum site, so that you can differentiate yourself from other applicants or other people in your program. I strongly ask you to reconsider this idea. If you work with autistic children for one year, and have no interest in the work, or do not plan on working with autistic children someday in your clinical practice, you will be losing a chance to gain meaningful clinical experience that can be applied to your clinical practice. This is a grave mistake. Please choose a practicum site that interests you, but which also has an application to your future. Don't choose a site just because it sounds cool, or because you think it would be cool to work with crisis patients. If you don't plan on doing psychotherapy with those struggling with schizophrenia in the future, don't choose a site that focuses its attention on thought disorders.

One of the most overwhelming parts of starting a practicum is starting to see patients for therapy. Whether you are doing group therapy or individual therapy, seeing your first patient as a second-year graduate student can be stressful. Having a good and empathic supervisor for this experience will help you gain strength. Remember that you are going to make mistakes throughout this process. Some mistakes are OK and are merely part of the learning process. I know I have made innumerable mistakes with patients whom I have seen for therapy. Your judgment and clinical inference is never going to be perfect. Sometimes, you will not understand their views or statements, and that will take years to improve. The idea with the practicum is that you gain valuable experience, gain insight, and learn from mistakes through clinical supervision. You want a supervisor who will not belittle you through this process, but who will help guide you in becoming a better and more competent therapist.

If you are doing group therapy in your practicum, simply reading Irvin D. Yalom's iconic text *The Theory and Practice of Group Psychotherapy* will help you learn from the master of group therapy. I know that this is a hard call, reading a book on top of your fulltime school and practicum site. But Yalom's writing style is engaging and easy to read. The book is a page-turner and it really won't take long. Leading a group can be overwhelming, but following Yalom's model will help you become more confident. Yalom also has a book that examines inpatient group therapy, and if you are working in a hospital setting, the text is also highly recommended. Group therapy is mentally satisfying and in the future you may want to incorporate group therapy into your clinical practice. I also think that learning about group therapy and group processes/dynamics will make you a more skilled individual therapist—and will make you a more financially successful private practice psychologist someday.

Internships

I can't say this strongly enough: if you do nothing else, challenge yourself by choosing internships that will give you a breadth of experience. This will prove invaluable to your career development. If you are really excited about working with children diagnosed with autistic spectrum disorders, take one internship on that. You don't want to have each internship doing the same thing. Choose other internships to make you more rounded. But also choose internships that are applicable to your future clinical practice. Don't just choose something because you find it to be interesting. Strongly consider having an internship working with work-injured or rehabilitation patients. Also consider working with pain patients, as these seem to be recent trends in terms of work opportunities. As the baby boomers grow older, I think this trend will continue, as more elderly people will have pain problems. Many will also have to look for work or keep working due to the current financial climate. Consider working with children, particularly evaluating children for cognitive and personality testing. This will allow you to be more financially successful as you build your private practice in the future, as evaluations with children (with some exceptions) usually pay better than those done with adults. Internships offer a multitude of non-monetary rewards in helping positively influence the lives of children or adolescents. Work with children is likely to be in increasing demand, as current research has yielded increased national attention to learning disabilities, developmental disorders and autistic spectrum disorders. If roughly one in 88 children is diagnosed with an autistic spectrum disorder, there are going to be many opportunities for the treatment and evaluation of those who are afflicted with these disorders. Working with child and adolescents is a good way to build a financially successful private practice in clinical psychology. And it feels good to work with children and to see them thrive while they are in treatment.

When you are selecting the internship, please speak to other students about the programs. Read the feedback that they have listed about the programs, but more importantly look online and speak to the former interns. If there are a few interns that have nothing but bad things to say about the program, then DO NOT SELECT THE PROGRAM. Check on the location of the internship as well. You don't want to select a program in a location where you will be miserable. For instance, you likely don't want to choose a crime-ridden place where you may be unsafe, or choose an internship that requires a one-hour commute each way. Do not select a program with a small stipend if you are going to be unhappy here. Your peers are going to be tremendous assets here. And the best thing is that the feedback and advice is free. Finding the right internship is really priceless. Some programs will require that you move out of state for the internship site, due to a dearth of sites. For instance, there are very few internship sites in the Seattle area, and many doctoral candidates need to have their internships out of state. So think about where your program is located and ask around before you start your program about the clinical internship opportunities in the area. There have been a number of Seattle-area doctoral students who have not been able to find internship sites in the Seattle area and have been forced to move 500 miles or more to complete their programs. So think about these potential problems before starting your doctoral program.

Feel out your supervisors when they are interviewing you. Your supervisors will likely be your references for recommendations in the future—which could open or close doors. The supervisor is an essential part of your internship position. When you are in the interview, if you have a bad feeling about the supervisors DO NOT TAKE THE INTERNSHIP. During the interview, you are interviewing the supervisor as well . . . they are not only interviewing you. You are going to be in there for a year with the supervisor, so it is essential that you relate well or at least relatively well with them. Check into the supervisor and find out about their background and experience. Choose a supervisor who has some experience with psychological testing. Psychological testing is going to make you better money out of grad school. Some internship sites will have multiple supervisors, such as a supervisor for therapy and a supervisor for psych testing. This was the case at my final internship site, a psychiatric hospital, where the lead supervisor was not familiar with psychological testing and so there was a second supervisor who was in charge of the psych testing cases. In this case, it is important for you to get to know both clinical supervisors. Make a huge effort to connect with your supervisor during the interview without being weird. Obviously, do not act like you know everything. Remember that you are the lowly intern. Know your place.

Ideally, you want to choose an internship site that has both psychological assessment and therapy. I would say that it would be highly recommended to find each internship site where that is an option. I was lucky that it was an option for my practicum and two internships. During my two internships, both therapy and assessment opportunities were very different as one was an outpatient clinic and the other was an inpatient psychiatric hospital. Obviously, the people whom I saw for therapy and assessment were very different. But both work opportunities offered a wide range of patients and psychological issues faced. I think that it is hard to place a value on seeing such a broad spectrum of the DSM IV TR, and you can really only see that by working at a crisis house or a psychiatric hospital. Some of the internship sites also offer various training opportunities. For instance, at my second internship site, we had presenters on different subjects in clinical psych, such as Dialectical-Behavior Therapy. These were great chances to learn something different that we weren't learning at the training site. You want to choose a site where you will become a strong diagnostician. Learning about diagnostics in a psychopathology class is important, but it is more important to become a strong diagnostician by receiving good clinical training and seeing a variety of mental health conditions. The proper supervision may greatly improve your ability to properly diagnose individuals.

Internship sites vary markedly in their degree of difficulty. Some are going to be more rigorous than others. Many of the psychiatric hospitals are competitive internship sites and offer strong training and more supervision opportunities. For instance, my psychiatric hospital site offered one hour of therapy supervision, one hour of assessment supervision, and two hours of group supervision each week, which offered tremendous opportunities to learn, not only from other interns but also from the supervisors. So the amount of supervision received is something to look into when you are choosing a clinical internship. Guidelines will also depend on your school's requirements. You don't want to find a bare-bones type of site or the type of site that doesn't offer the right amount of supervision and has a supervisor who will just sign off on your hours. I have heard from various colleagues who were disenchanted by their supervisor's lack of efforts and time supervising the interns, and you don't want to be stuck in that situation, lacking learning opportunities. Some of my greatest learning opportunities, from both psychological testing and therapy, came from individual supervision time at my practicum and internship sites. If you are interested in teaching someday, consider finding a site where the supervisor has teaching experience and can help you learn more about instruction or presenting. For instance, opportunities for presenting case studies may help you become a more accomplished orator and may greatly improve your ability to convey your message—and may improving your teaching skills.

You want to be thinking about internship sites that will make you financially successful someday. As indicated earlier, internships in which you work with children may lead to a highly rewarding and financially successful career direction in the future. If you feel adventurous, and are interested in the brain, choose a neuropsychological internship. Neuropsychology is another sub-discipline in psychology that offers financial success and also separates what you do from other professions. Here you might want to think about internships where you work with traumatic brain-injury patients, autistic spectrum disorders, and other neurological disorders. Once you are out of grad school, neuropsychological evaluations pay pretty much the best out of all evaluations. Typically, insurance companies pay the highest rates for these evaluations, so that is something to consider. With reimbursement rates dwindling in the helping professions, it is good to know that you can potentially make a good living doing neuropsych evaluations.

Getting Through Grad School

This section's title seems quite vague so I will do my best to explain. What it should be titled is "you need to finish graduate school ASAP." Not to put any added pressure on you or anything. Now, I know, you just got into a great school. You are super cool. That is not a small feat. Usually for most doctoral-level programs, fewer than 20 percent are admitted into the program. Swallow your pride for one second.

Now that you got in, work hard. Work your ass off. This is going to mean fewer Coronas and tequila shots. It is going to mean fewer movies and more moves on cognitive-behavioral therapy techniques. It means fewer weekend getaways and more weekend study breaks. I am not saying that you should push to finish your program in three years. That is likely impossible. But it does mean you need to set a goal to complete your program in four or five years (five years at the latest). If you work diligently, you should have no problem in completing your program in five years. There has been compelling evidence that suggests it is easier today to complete a doctoral program than ever before. In 2004, the APA Council of Graduate Schools began a PhD Completion Project, researching completion rates among doctoral candidates. The research indicated that in 1992, 65 percent of doctoral students in psychology had completed their program within 10 years. Ten years is brutal and doctoral programs have acted to benefit grad students. Programs are becoming more focused on helping students finish their programs in a timely fashion. Some examples include providing peer support networks, improved medical leave, improving student networking, encouraging students to begin research earlier, and offering mentoring and advising (Winerman, 2008).

My program offered academic advising, particularly through my first two years of the program. I found that the program was helpful, although it was at first somewhat scary being in a room with a professor and talking about my academic plan. The advising meetings became less scary as I learned more about my advisor. I was lucky enough to have an advisor who was warm and insightful. So I would say that my school's advising program helped my progress through the first few years of the program and also helped me to graduate quickly.

You don't want anything to slow you down as you progress through graduate school. But let's say that your program is paid for by your parents or through scholarships. That may be less of a reason to graduate quickly, as you will not have as much as a financial incentive to complete the program in a timely fashion. But if your program is not paid for, as mine was not, you are going to have to pay a substantial tuition. Factor in housing costs and this could land you out more than $40K if you end up finishing in five years rather than four years. That is a huge sum of money. You can save so much money by graduating early.

What I am saying is that it is in your best interest to get out of school, work hard on licensing, and start your practice ASAP. If your state requires postdoctoral hours, that is going to set you back another year. And it will cause further financial burden. If you don't have to do that, as I didn't (thank you, glorious State of Washington), then you will be closer to being on your way to making some real money. Washington does not require postdoctoral hours, but some states will require up to 1,500 hours.

Some requirements will encumber you. It will be a major pain taking an extra class every semester. So don't do that every semester. Do it every other semester. Some programs do not require you to be in class during the summer, but you should really do summer school if you can. This is going to save you a ton of money in the long run and will also get you through school more quickly. Don't take a heavy course load in the summer; just take some. Stay busy. This will be to your benefit in the future. You also don't want to overwhelm yourself during the summer. That should be your time to recharge and get ready for the next academic year.

Make friends in your program. No doubt your program has some really good and interesting people. Maybe it doesn't. But it is very likely that there are some people there who think just like you, with the same worldviews and opinions, and share some of the same interests. I can remember when I went down to San Diego I didn't know anyone down there. It was rather an onerous feeling to be alone and not have friends in the close vicinity. All of my close friends were back in the Pacific Northwest. I remember thinking one day that while I have some great friends up north, I really should make friends while I am in San Diego. I put myself out there. To make friends, you will have to do the same. Attend the social gatherings, talk to other students, and really make an effort. You will likely be glad that you did. I have made some amazing, lifelong friends from my program. These are people whom I contact regularly for consultation/venting sessions. They make my life better.

Friendships are also a great way of helping cope through the trials and tribulations of grad school. You are going to have some tough times and it is great to have good friends to connect with. They will be able to give you useful advice. They will tell you about a professor they liked or didn't like. They will help you through a breakup of a romantic relationship. They will tell you about the internship site that you absolutely should not apply for. There are too many reasons not to make an effort to form friendships in graduate school. I definitely felt a nice sense of camaraderie with my friends and colleagues in my program. Your friends from graduate school may also be great people to consult with in the future, so there is future value here as well.

Choosing a Dissertation Chair

This can be a major reason why you graduate in five years or why you graduate in seven years. Choosing your dissertation chair will depend on your doctoral program. Sometimes, the program chooses your chair for you or pushes you to use a particular dissertation chair. My program did not make each person choose a particular chair. But you should choose someone with whom you have done research with our have taken classes. Don't choose someone who you took classes from and didn't like or who didn't inspire you. Choose someone whose classes you have enjoyed or whose current/recent research excites you. Some of my classmates wanted a particular dissertation chair but were turned down because the chair was too busy or the chair disagreed with the research ideas that the student was postulating. You want to begin your search for your dissertation chair right when you begin grad school. In the first two years, you should be thinking about who might be a good fit for you. Most programs require a dissertation class. So in your first year, and definitely in your second year, you need to think about which classes seem appealing to you. This would not be a good time to just take a dissertation class because your friend wants you to. If you begin a dissertation class and are thinking that the instructor would not make a good chair, or if you have another chair in mind, try to switch your class. This also happened to a few colleagues of mine, and they ended up with the dissertation chair that they wanted.

Completing the dissertation takes years, depending on your initiative, writing abilities, and other factors. You can spend more than three years of time on your dissertation if you are unlucky and do not work hard enough. Once you have completed your coursework and you are ABD (All But Dissertation), a lot of your time is going to based on what your dissertation chair is like. There are many questions to consider. Here are some:

Is he/she working hard to get you graduated and completed? Do they care about your progress? How long do they take to get the revisions back? What is their schedule like? Do they have seven kids and ten grandchildren? Do they take regular two-month vacations? How do you generally get along with your chair? What is your relationship with them like? These are some questions that you might want to ask about.

Obviously, you want to choose a chair with whom you relate well, because you are going to be seeing them regularly for the next year or two. My dissertation chair was a hilarious man from New York. He was very proud of his heritage and he spoke with a heavy New York accent. Dr. Madero was mainly interested in psych testing, but also had some other interests, such as school violence, which was also important to me. Dr. Madero was a wise man who had a ton of funny stories . . . some which might have bordered on being inappropriate. That didn't bother me. We connected well, where he might not have vibed as well with others who were more sensitive. While I never asked him, I think he respected me. I let him know that I respected him.

Dr. Madero went out of his way to help me on many occasions. I let him know that. He would sometimes invite me and others from our dissertation class for BBQs and movie nights. The man was a hockey fanatic and we talked hockey. We would both lament the progress, or lack of progress, of our favorite teams. Dr. Madero would help me on the weekends and he knew that I was working hard on my dissertation. Sometimes he would get frustrated at me for having spelling errors, which was infuriating at the time but is downright hilarious looking back. Hey, the man had some obsessive tendencies . . . he always wanted the classroom a certain way and we had to arrange it as such. I had a great experience with my dissertation chair, but I have heard countless nightmares about people and their chairs. For instance, I have heard of chairs not returning their dissertation drafts for months. I had a friend who didn't get his dissertation back for more than a month. This really slowed down his graduation process. Guess what—those people probably didn't do the research when they were selecting their chairs. Please, do the research on this one. Call your colleagues and ask them about the prospective chairs. Put a call in to someone who you think might be a good chair for you. You are going to be spending a lot of time with your chair . . . make sure that you choose a good one. Take the initiative to try to get to know your dissertation chair. You are going to need to set up meetings and do many things on your own. Some chairs might help with some hand-holding and others may not. But you can't expect dissertation chairs to do many things for you.

Some people may be tempted to take some time off during graduate school. Maybe you received a job offer or want to take time off to think about whether you want to be a psychologist. In my opinion, this is work that you should have done before you started grad school. Now that you are here, I strongly encourage you to just finish the degree. Unless you are in your first year or maybe your second year, I don't recommend taking time off, unless you are thinking of a two-week vacation. You definitely don't want to take a year off, because that will severely impede your progress. Some people might have the idea that they will work better on their dissertation if they are writing in the south of France or in Barcelona. I think those ideas are utopian rather than reasonable. Some of the most respected voices in completing graduate school, such as Dr. John Norcross have noted that it is important to work on the dissertation while you are living close to your school. He notes that living further away from school is a good reason to procrastinate and lose your focus.

It is essential that you complete the dissertation. You never know what kind of job you might be doing someday. The degree may come in handy whether you are wanting to join the police force in the future as a supervisor, whether you want to get into politics, or other various fields. A doctoral degree in psychology has a good amount of carryover into other professions. But unless you have a job offer that you cannot refuse, strongly consider just pushing through the program. I would say that pretty much any job offer is not a good enough reason to fail to complete your doctoral program. If you are having some serious mental health issues and are very unhappy, that may be a good reason to leave the program. In that case, please consider seeing a psychologist to help yourself. There is a certain healthiness of persevering through a doctoral program and doing things that are difficult and taxing but not impossible. The mountain ahead of you in your first year may seem insurmountable, but as you build steam through the second and third years, you come closer and closer to the apex. Sooner or later you will be at the summit, looking down at the beautiful scenery. You will feel winded, but proud of your accomplishment.

Completing the Dissertation

You hear about these people who are ABD, which basically means that they have completed all of their coursework and only need to complete the dissertation. Sometimes, it is difficult to continue to work hard. Many students procrastinate. In fact, recent research has suggested that roughly 80 to 95 percent of college students procrastinate (Steel, 2007).

It might make sense that those who do not procrastinate also report lower levels of stress and illness than those who admit to procrastinating (Tice & Baumeister, 2007). These reports are consistent with some of my colleagues who have noted that they felt more stressed out toward the end of their program when they were delaying the inevitable and procrastinating on working on their dissertation. Of the students who have finished their coursework, how many people finish the dissertation? Well, research from 1992 indicates that roughly 80 percent of those who have finished their doctoral-level coursework in Psychology complete their dissertation. I don't know about you, but this number seems pretty scary. This means that one in five students have already completed all of their coursework but will not complete the dissertation. That is way too many people, if you ask me. Dr. John Norcross is an expert on getting into graduate school programs and also completing them. Norcross has mentioned that there are some key points to completing the dissertation. He recommends creating a schedule, which sets up deadlines for each part of the dissertation (Deangelis, 2010).

This is a bit more regimented than what I did, but for those who lack self-discipline, it seems like a bright idea. Norcross also recommends completing your dissertation before you finish your internship.

This may be possible, depending on your program. I know that this would not be possible for my program, since the dissertation class started our third year and our first internship started our third year. Norcross recommends this strategy particularly if your internship is far from your school, because it will be harder to complete the dissertation if you do not to have the constant contact with your school. Finally, Norcross recommends finding a solid support network. This is what I have been saying throughout this manuscript. It is essential to have a good support network in completing your program in a timely fashion. Whether it is a group of friends, a spouse, or people from church, having a close connection of people to discuss your journey and difficult process will help you complete the voyage.

Preparing for the Defense

Only a few things to offer on this one. I am someone who enjoys public speaking, but I am probably talking about pulling teeth for those who have presentation anxiety. If you have presentation anxiety, please work on it in therapy or read about it. Over prepare for the defense, because you don't want to have to re-do the dissertation if you haven't done a good job. There will probably be people watching your defense. Prepare for that. Pretend that the president is there. There are a few people who will fail the defense, but most tend to fail because they are unfamiliar with their statistics. If you are doing quantitative research, be sure to know your statistics and theories. If you can't defend your statistics, you might not pass. If you have trouble with understanding the statistics, consider consulting with a statistician. Think about the tests that you used and why you used them. You also want to consider hypotheticals for your test data. For instance, my dissertation chair was an expert on the Rorschach Inkblot Test. So, not surprisingly, I deduced that he would likely ask me questions about the Rorschach regarding my test data and populations studied. He did, and I was able to respond adequately because I had prepared. Since my dissertation was on the Minnesota Multiphasic Personality Inventory, Second Edition (MMPI-2), I knew that there would be questions asked about the test and potentially about related tests, such as the Millon-2 or 3. So I prepared for the hypothetical questions, whether they were asked or not.

Remember that many people who are there will be there because they don't want to be. They probably don't care a lick about what you are talking about. Most people who attend presentations don't listen to the content. They are probably thinking about themselves or thinking about what they are having for lunch. They are not interested in hearing about T-scores, normative data, or literature reviews. The presentation is a lot easier when you recognize that people are not attentively listening to your every word. The thought that they are attentively listening is just a distortion. And what do you do with distortions? You throw them aside and change them to something that is truer! Prepare hard and practice. You will do great!

References

DeAngelis, T. (2010). Fear not. *Grad Psych*, September, 38. Retrieved from http://www.apa.org/gradpsych/2010/09/cover-fear.aspx

Steel, P. (2007). The nature of procrastination: A meta-analytic and theoretical review of quintessential self-regulatory failure. *Psychological Bulletin*, *133*(1), 65–94.

Tice, D. & Baumeister, R. (2007). Longitudinal study of procrastination, performance, stress, and health: The costs and benefits of dawdling. *Psychological Science, 8*(6), 454–458.

U.S. Department of Education. (2006, June 18). Research doctorate programs. Retrieved from www.ed.gov

Winerman, L. (2008). Ten years to a doctorate? Not anymore. *Grad Psych*. Retrieved from http://www.apa.org/gradpsych/2008/03/cover-doctorate.aspx

5

LIFE AFTER GRADUATE SCHOOL

On EPPP

Congratulations for defending your dissertation. Get a few things signed off and you will officially be a doctor. So you are there. Now what? Guess what, you have a huge test to study for. I mean huge. And even worse, you cannot start your practice until you pass the EPPP (Examination for the Professional Practice of Psychology). In many states, you will also have a state exam to take. Usually, the state exams are easier than the EPPP, so I am not going to discuss them. Some state exams are rather easy, while some other states are considerably more difficult. You might want to do some more research on the state examinations, depending on what state you want to begin your private practice.

The EPPP is a laborious hurdle to overcome. When I was taking the exam, there was about a 55 percent pass rate. Now the test board indicates that about 80 percent of those taking the exam for the first time pass. My program has had about 65 percent pass in the past five years. Some other programs come in around a 50 percent pass rate. The test board recommends a score of 500, which is roughly 70 percent on the exam. The exam is comprised of the following domains: Biological Basis of Behavior: 11 percent; Cognitive-Affective Basis of Behavior: 13 percent; Social and Multicultural Basis of Behavior: 12 percent; Growth and Lifespan Development: 13 percent; Assessment and Diagnosis: 14 percent; Treatment, Intervention, Prevention: 15 percent; Research Methods and Statistics: 7 percent; Ethical/Legal/ Professional Issues: 15 percent. Now, this exam has changed slightly since I took it in 2008, but it is basically similarly structured. While

I can't comment on my performance or offer any specific opinion, I would say that one thing to do is make sure that you know all about statistics. Now I know you are asking, "Why, that doesn't make any sense. Statistics encompasses only 7 percent of the exam." I know that there will not be a ton of statistics questions. My program definitely did not focus on statistics. But I'm telling you, if you have your statistics completely covered, you will see a stats question and whiz through it. With the stats questions, there will only be one good answer . . . if you know stats, you are going to know the answer immediately. This will help you power through the long exam and will save you a ton of time if you know the answer right away. Not only will it save you time, you will feel good that you know the correct response right away. There will be so many questions on the EPPP where the right answer won't come at you right away, so having your stats down cold will help you with both time and confidence. Remember that you don't have to achieve perfect scores on every section of the exam. Some of the sections are going to be easier and others will be more difficult. Try to figure out where your problem areas are and focus on improving your scores in those areas. For instance, I had not reviewed statistics for many years. While I had a good grasp on diagnostics and case vignettes, I needed serious review on stats. But with hard work, statistics became one of my strengths for the exam.

Now some more advice. Whatever you do, please purchase the testing materials on the exam. These books/audio CDs are made by people who only focus on having you prepare for the exam. Consider listening to the CDs whenever you can. You can just put them into your iPod or MP3 player, and they will be wherever you are. Good times, huh? What I like about utilizing the CDs is that it involves a different form of learning, through auditory processing. I also think that the CDs serve as a nice contrast to just reading the materials over and over again. You are going to get very bored studying, so any change in format might make studying slightly less mundane. Those who create the materials want you to pass and create the study materials to help you learn what you need to know for the exam.

Probably the best advice I can give is to take the four-day course on the exam. My former supervisor recommended that I take the class on the EPPP and I was glad that I did. I, as well as many of my colleagues, recommend the Association for Advanced Training in the Behavioral Sciences (AATBS) workshop. Regarding the workshop, a female colleague concurred, stating that the workshop was, "The best money that I ever spent." Both the instructors that I had were fantastic. One of the instructors was a former professor of mine, Dr. Ellen Stein. Dr. Stein is so incredibly intelligent and entertaining that she can make a statistics review fun. I'm not lying, she has some really hilarious jokes . . . just what you need when you're sitting in a classroom for eight hours learning about statistics. The other instructor, Dr. Michael Kerner, was an outstanding orator and gave some great inside information about the exam. I highly recommend that you take this class. And no, I was not paid by AATBS to say this! Look, I know that taking the class and buying the study materials cost money. They are very expensive. But they are worth the money. Probably combined, the class and materials are $2K. Once you have your practice, you will earn back that money in a flash. Just see 20 therapy patients at $100 a pop or see 15 at $150 a pop. Borrow money or take out a loan, but whatever you do make sure to buy the materials that you need to succeed. The exam is too important not to make the proper preparations. Also consider finding a mentor during this period to "talk shop" with. The mentor will keep your mind active in clinical psychology and will be supportive of you starting a new practice. The mentor also will have some good advice for when you have finally finished the exams.

I would treat studying for the exam from a behavioral perspective. Consider sectioning off time each day to study for the exam. For instance, if your schedule will allow, spend one or two hours per day studying. Just put your studying on the calendar and treat it as an appointment. You might want to set up a system of rewards and punishments for completing or not completing your studying, giving yourself a tangible reward each week for completing a week's worth of daily studying. Rewards might be a trip to the movies, dinner out with your significant other, or taking in a sporting event or concert. If you don't complete your studying, you don't get your reward at the end of the week. It will be up to you to hold yourself accountable. Your best friend or significant other can also help in holding you accountable to your studying goal.

Studying for the EPPP takes time and hard work. It is not the type of exam that you can just take after graduate school, regardless of the quality of education that you have received. If you put in the hard time, you will likely get positive results.

Licensure

Before taking the EPPP, you need to consider what state or states that you want to be licensed in. Each state has different licensure requirements, so you should really consider where you want to live before you begin graduate school. Some required classes for licensure vary by state. This can be a major roadblock if you decide that you want to move out of state and your program does not have the classes required by the state. I have a colleague who had to go back to graduate school because she moved to a state where she didn't meet all of the class requirements for licensure. You need to consider these things before you start graduate school, because you don't want to waste a lot of time and money as my colleague did.

Also, the predoctoral and postdoctoral hours vary by state. So think about those requirements before you apply for licensure. If you are considering licensure on the East Coast, know that many East Coast States require accredited predoctoral and postdoctoral internships. Some states will require either an APA or Association of Psychology Postdoctoral and Internship Centers (APPIC) internship. Some states require a postdoc, while others do not. The postdoc will be your last chance to gain supervision and learn about the business side of things before you start your private practice. I have had colleagues who have not met their state's required hours and had to go back and gain supervised hours, which is also just wasting time and money. If you plan on completing a postdoc, you want to try finding a supervisor who knows about the business side of practice. The supervisor of one of my colleagues was a private-practice psychologist and she mentioned that she learned a great deal about billing, starting a practice, and other invaluable intangibles while she was at her postdoc placement. Some of the postdoc supervisors may be in academics and might be supportive, but won't know about the business side of practice. So you want to consider these issues before you choose a postdoc site.

Once You Are Licensed

Congrats, you have passed. You are now licensed. This is a huge accomplishment. Make sure to reward yourself. Consider taking a short vacation to somewhere warm. Or maybe that road trip that you've always wanted to do. Whatever you do, DO NOT TAKE A TWO-MONTH VACATION. I know that you want to really reward yourself now that you have passed and are licensed. But the bills are going to pile up. Student loans are going to set in. Do not take an opulent vacation with money that you don't have. I have heard about those who are licensed and take huge backpacking trips around Europe with money that they don't have. Hey, if your parents give you the money, please do take advantage of it . . . use it to freaking start your practice. Because starting a practice is going to be expensive. Do not waste your money on a lavish vacation. That being said, there is nothing wrong with doing something rewarding, like a wine-tasting weekend, or seeing a great musical. But do not blow a ton of money now that you are licensed. You will thank me later.

Welcome to the real world (hard slap to face). Now get ready to make some money. You are going to need to talk to a lawyer about starting up a business. Make sure to look into phone and internet, and you are going to need to think about the office location. Again, think about giving yourself some type of intrinsic reward for passing your exam. A nice weekend trip might do the trick. Or maybe think about a trip to the spa. Then get back and focused.

6

STARTING YOUR PRIVATE PRACTICE

Finding a Financial Advisor

I would highly recommend hiring a financial advisor. We didn't go to school to learn about the financial world. Just as we didn't go to school for bookkeeping. We didn't learn about stocks and bonds and mutual funds. OK, there are the rare people in our field who are good at everything. I get that. But come on—are you really a great financial analyst? Are you going to do as well as a seasoned financial analyst? With rare exceptions, I would say your response is going to be a resounding no! I definitely took an interest in finance when I was in grad school. My dad taught me a good deal about business and also world financial markets. I learned enough about it but didn't learn enough about it to make it my living. My advisor did. He has been in the field for 20 years and helped me do very well last year with my mutual funds. I tried playing the stocks a bit when I first started my practice. Yeah, that was nearly a disaster. I knew a little bit and probably thought that I knew more than I did. After losing some money with the Washington Mutual meltdown (that everyone predicted WOULDN'T happen), I decided to throw in the towel. Playing the stocks is like gambling. Sometimes you win big and sometimes you lose big. I didn't lose a ton of money but it was an eye-opener that I need to have a real professional handling my money.

So check into the people who have a reputation in your city or town. Don't just go to the local Edward Jones office. Go interview a few people. Consider calling a few firms such as Merrill Lynch, or Charles Schwab, to get a feel for the person that they recommend you see. It is important to have some face time with the person that they recommend. Consider getting recommendations from people who are financially successful. Ask friends or colleagues if they know about the advisor and ask about their reputation around town. I went with someone I knew I could trust and who had a good reputation. Talk to the prospective advisors and candidly ask them about their results. Ask them how they did in the financial disaster of 2008. Ask them how much a typical client lost in mutual funds. Make sure to have them tell you about individual success stories. Ask if they have ever managed a psychologist's or other doctor's money. This is a little bit like choosing a therapist or hiring someone for your business. You want to find someone who is a good fit for you. Do not choose someone who is going to retire right away, because you are going to have to go through the same boring selection process once again. I would choose someone who has an office that is relatively close to your office. I wouldn't choose someone in New York if you live in L.A. You want to go in and talk to these people from time to time about investment opportunities, and it is better to do that in person than over the phone. Ask friends or colleagues if they know about the advisor and ask about their reputation around town. My work with my financial analyst has been an excellent experience thus far.

Office and Location

It is essential to find a great office to start your private practice in psychology. The last thing you want when you are starting out is to have a high overhead. For the non-econ majors, overhead refers to expenses such as rent, lighting, internet, etc. You want to find the best value out there that has the lowest overhead but is in a decent location. If you find a place that is dirty and in a run-down building, your office is going to reflect negatively on you. You want to be somewhere that people expect of a professional. You also want a location where patients are going to feel safe and comfortable. Think about calling a few psychologists and talking to them about locations. Most of them will be candid. You will want to have some nice colleagues in the area.

I chose an office location in an older building that was close to other psychologists in the area but was in the financial center of the town.

This is in one of the nicest parts of town and is close to Starbucks, banks, and shopping. The part of the town is renovated to look more modern. There are decent restaurants around my office as well (important for lunch breaks). Please, choose a great bargain in a decent location. I know you want to find somewhere hip and cool, but honestly that won't matter and it won't give you financial gain. Don't do that. You will just be wasting money on overhead and you will have to work more and harder than you want to in order to cover the overhead. Now, that is not to say that you can't move to a beautiful building once you have saved thousands of dollars and have a full practice. But when you are starting out, being in the hip location is just not worth it. Local and state organizations, as well as the APA monitor, may also have information about office spaces, so that might be a good place to start looking as well.

The other important thing to consider is choosing an office location that is not saturated with psychologists. For instance, when I left San Diego for the Seattle area, I left in part knowing that San Diego has one of the highest (if not the highest) percentages of psychologists living in the area. There are just a ton of psychologists down there. And that doesn't make for good business opportunities. Business is about supply and demand. There is demand for mental health providers down there but there is too large a supply, in my opinion.

When I moved back to Seattle, I chose an office about 30 minutes north of the city in a town called Everett. This made perfect sense. First, I grew up in the town. Second, I knew that there were not that many psychologists practicing there. I did my research to find out who was there and how many psychologists were in the town and surrounding areas. Turned out that the town was somewhat underserved by psychologists. I knew there was going to be a need. It made perfect sense. I also knew in the Seattle-proper area that there were a plethora of psychologists, which would mean fewer opportunities for me. While I could charge a higher hourly rate in Seattle, I couldn't charge considerably higher. And I wanted things to get started; I wanted to become established and so my location outside of the city made sense. Setting up shop in Everett has been a true blessing, as much of my family is in the town and I see them regularly. I have coffee breaks with friends from high school and chat with attorney friends down the street. My location outside of the city, in something of an underserved area, has been one of the best decisions in terms of becoming established. It has been a great money-making opportunity. There are some major advantages to starting a practice in a place where you already have connections. For instance, if you have lived your first 18 years in Tampa, Florida, it is likely that you already have some connections and potential referrals out there. And this book is about making money, not living in the trailer park.

I want to offer some other ideas for starting your office. Please consider cutting corners by buying your furniture on Craigslist or another relatively cheap website. Remember, you are going to have to purchase expensive psychological tests so DO NOT spend your money on expensive furniture, rugs, or pricey office decor. I was trying to convince a friend/colleague not to do this. He told me that his parents were going to loan him some money to have some nice office furniture. If you are in this situation, then still don't buy the nice furniture. I am assuming that he will have to pay his parents back. Focus on spending your money on essentials such as psychological assessment instruments. That is paramount. Having the new Restoration Hardware couch is not. If you work with children, you might want to consider having a washable rug or washable furniture. Remember that kids can be messy, and they likely will be bringing drinks and snacks into your office, so you will likely want to have things that you can wash. Also, you might want to have kid-friendly furniture if you work with kids. If you do psychological testing with children, consider buying toys so that the kids can play with something during the clinical interview.

Consider having good lighting in your office. It is going to help, especially if you are going to be seeing patients later in the evening. And sometimes you will have to see them after five p.m. . . . fact of life. I know your mom just bought the new couch. Maybe your significant other thinks that it will be a good idea. I don't care, don't buy it. It will be wasted money. You need to have a nice, functional office. That does not mean that you need to have an elaborate or opulent office. Have a nice lamp, a table, and a couch, and consider having another chair in there for an alternative seating area. Hey, sometimes people just want to sit in the chair, not the couch. I bought my stuff on Craigslist and it was all IKEA stuff. So far, the purchased furniture has lasted me more than five years and has held up quite nicely. I suggest including a moderate-sized area rug in a warm color, particularly a shade of muted red, as a mentor suggested for me.

Now my waiting area does have some nice furniture. It is not expensive furniture but it is good, comfy seating for people. I have tried to create a relaxing environment for patients, attempting to lower their stress levels for starting therapy/evaluations. Consider having some plants in there that might create a relaxing garden theme. Or hopefully it will remind them of a relaxing garden . . . that's what you hope, right? I have had some positive feedback about the plants in my office, so I think I am on the right track there. I have pictures of my travels up on the wall as well as some relaxing (non-chaotic) art. I just try to create a soothing environment, and you should, too. In my waiting area, there are many comfortable places to sit. I encourage people to relax. I also have bottled water in my fridge. I know this seems extravagant but it is super cheap at Costco. And sometimes people just want a freebie like that. Plus, you are giving something that is good for them. Strongly consider giving something for free. It doesn't have to be bottled water but it can be a candy basket with individually wrapped mints. People like these small things for free and it can really make your place inviting. Having many places to sit in your waiting room is important, because you are going to have more than one person waiting, I guarantee it. Another thing to consider in conjunction with this is having some room in your waiting room. Have you ever sat in a small, cramped waiting room where the body odor of the person next to you is unbearable? If your waiting room is spacious and people are not crammed together, this will remedy that. If you can avoid it, don't have your office in a small, confined waiting room. This is going to cause further duress for those who are coming to see you for the first time and are already stressed out about it.

Please also consider having some decent magazines in the office. This will also contribute to a relaxed environment for your patients. Do you remember going to the doctor or dentist's office when you were a kid? Remember going to those who had some really good magazines?

What did you think about that? They were great, weren't they? Now do you remember the really run-down offices with no magazines? There was nothing to do in them, they were deemed "run down," and it contributed to a less-than-satisfactory experience. In terms of magazines, consider having a bunch of different ones. I know I am talking about cutting costs, but there are some insignificant costs. Consider *Men's Health, Vogue,* and the dreaded *People* (only because it costs an arm and a leg). I think *People* is the number-one magazine to have. The main reason to get this magazine is it is light reading. The second main reason is that it comes EVERY week! Get it. It is worth the money and the money that you spend on your magazines is a write-off, business expense. You can also get the "professional rate" on your subscription. There are also a ton of cheap magazines that arrive on a monthly basis, so look into those as well and find some good ones. Don't subscribe only to *Yachting* or *Field and Stream,* because of the narrow focus of the publications. These are details but it can make a difference for your patients.

Finally, you will need to find a location where you can place your records. I have a small, locked room that I reserve for my records. I have seen some other psychologists place their records in their room for testing or therapy, but I feel that if it is possible, it is best to have a separate room for records. The fact is that I have such a high volume of patients and have seen so many testing patients that their records end up occupying a large amount of space. So I really wouldn't have enough room in my office to store all of their files. Eventually, depending on the state, you will need to carefully expunge your records. Be sure to check your state requirements on keeping records.

Also essential to a financially successful private practice in clinical psychology is a strong informed consent form. You will also need to have a good intake form and informed consent form for both therapy and testing patients. The intake form should have essentials, such as date of birth, phone numbers, and emergency contact numbers. Consult with colleagues in choosing a good intake form. With the informed consent form, it is essential that you take your time and review the state laws for reasons for breaking confidentiality. Include any special topics in the informed consent form. For instance, I see a good deal of work-injured patients for therapy, so I have a special

section on work-injured patients. Also consider a section on your poli-
cies regarding social networking and communication by phone and
email. Make sure to have at least two colleagues review your informed
consent forms for therapy and testing. They can give you good candid
feedback and can help correct any errors that you may have. Be open to
the feedback that they give you and take your time creating a mistake-
free document. With your testing informed consent document, be sure
to explain who the referral source is (for instance, whether the referral
is from an organization or from an individual) and also have boxes to
check which type of evaluation you are conducting. This is important
to review with the client, because they might not know whether you
are giving them a cognitive assessment, a personality assessment, a
clinical interview, or some other type of evaluation.

Hiring a Bookkeeper

First of all, I didn't want to hire someone when I began my practice. I
was thinking, "I'm competent; I can do this on my own. I won't really
need anyone managing my books." I was dead wrong. Please do this.
There is really no reason not to. Let's begin with some simple math.
I am going to say that my time is worth at the least $100 an hour. Did
you learn Quickbooks when you were in grad school? Did you learn
really anything about bookkeeping? My hunch says that you didn't. Not
that the program is incredibly difficult to learn, but it takes at the bare
minimum of a few hours to become familiar with it. So you have spent
$200 essentially paying for the software and now you have to try to learn
the program. You also want someone to manage your books. Please do
not do this unless you do it very effortlessly and quickly. You are going
to be wasting your money if you do. Now, if you pay a bookkeeper at
$25 per hour, you would only be out $50. That $200 minus $50 equals
one fantastic dinner out. Or some groceries. Or a trip to Costco. That
$150 every month also means $1,800 per year. Now that equates to
many great dinners. Or it is a fantastic vacation. Whatever you do, hire
a bookkeeper. This will equate to money in your pocket.

Bookkeepers already know how to use the software. They are familiar
with the software and the practices of bookkeeping. I asked around when

I was looking for a bookkeeper. I ended up finding someone who was highly recommended by my accountant. My accountant had said that this person was looking for extra work for small businesses and I interviewed her and chose her. She has done a great job for me. Make sure to interview the person who is managing your books. You will want to find someone who is experienced and someone you can trust with all of your receipts. I do a great deal of state and government work, as well as insurance work, so having a ton of receipts can be tough to work through. She does this on a daily basis and it is no problem for her. She doesn't even ask me to organize everything. You want to hire someone who is tech savvy, because some of the states require you to file taxes online.

At a minimum, you want someone who has been doing bookkeeping for a few years. Ask them if they are familiar with the tax systems in your state. For instance, in Washington State, we have this lovely tax called "Business and Operations," also known as B and O. Every business owner has to pay B and O tax on a monthly or quarterly system. I pay quarterly. My bookkeeper takes care of it, tells me how much I owe, and then I write my check. Also ask how much money they charge. I am thinking that $20–30 an hour is reasonable. If they say $50 or $100 an hour, regardless of how experienced or competent they are, I would steer clear. You want to find someone who is already working a 9–5 job. This shows that the person is reliable. Honestly, they are not going to be putting in an enormous amount of work for you, anyway. The most that my bookkeeper has worked at a time is 10 hours. I have my bookkeeper manage my books four times a year (quarterly), and pay her about $100 to $200 per visit. This is a business expense, by the way (I will come to business expenses). So be sure to find someone who is both reasonably priced and reliable. Make sure to treat your biller nicely because they are the ones who are collecting much of your money. You want them to be happy and then they will do the best work for you.

Business Expenses

I should really do a better job of managing my business expenses. Honestly, there is so much that you can write off as a business owner. People I know have written off football tickets and cars. To my knowledge, the

IRS is really cracking down on business expenses that are superfluous, so I will only have a few things to add here. For instance, you can't put a new car as a business expense, as there are very strict parameters for such expenditures.

My first recommendation is don't do anything stupid that will get you audited. You have made it, you are licensed, and you are excited. Don't buy a boat, thinking that it will be a write-off. A car, however, can be a partial write-off if you are using your car to drive around to do psych evals. I do that, so my car ends up being a partial write-off. Not that I get a ton back on it, but it works a little in my favor. But this also goes back to my spending argument that people should not buy expensive things that they cannot afford when they are starting out. Don't buy the uber-expensive car thinking that it will be a write-off. That's not the way that the IRS works.

Stamps, stationery, and business cards are all business expenses. Phone and internet are business expenses. Dinners with colleagues are also business expenses. These are excellent opportunities to consult. I regularly have lunches and dinners with colleagues, as these are great chances to talk about ethical and professional issues while enjoying a good steak. Go ahead; choose the nicer restaurant in this case. Also, consider taking a trip to somewhere new to attend a conference. The whole thing is a business expense, including meals. I am going to Europe this summer and will be writing off a portion of the trip, as I will attend some training opportunities for continuing education. I strongly urge you to do this. Take advantage of the tax opportunities that you do have. I have also taken trips to Southern California to consult with colleagues and have used a portion of the trip as a business expense. Folks, this is a good idea. Consider creative ways to manage business expenses. Come on, you know that you want to go to that Forensic Psychology conference in Barbados!

Creating a Website

You will need to create a website. The website doesn't have to be the most technically advanced or beautiful thing in the world. It needs to have useful and accurate information about you. Consider using Siteskins.

com. They do an excellent job with customer service and they have some good ideas. You get a template from there and just basically type in the information that you want to have on your website. Sounds pretty easy, huh? You don't need to have amazing computer skills to create one.

My website is simple, with a few pictures and information about myself and my practice. It has some of my philosophy about therapy and psych testing. It has my rates, my background, and my vita. It also has an embedded news clip of me discussing school violence. Consider having similar things on your website. I have a blog on my website which also has some good, hopefully practical, information on psychological issues. For instance, I have small blurbs about things from presentation anxiety to seasonal affective disorder. Do not have someone do it for you, because you will be wasting money. It is actually quite a fun and easy project. People are going to ask you about your website and you will look dumb if you tell them that you don't have one. This is also a great way to break the ice for new therapy patients. Patients have told me consistently that viewing my website to find out information about me and my background has cut down on iatrogenic anxiety (nervousness about beginning therapy). The website can be a nice asset for you. I'd urge you to have your website address on your business cards. The website is going to be an extension of you, so don't do anything too strange or wild. I have gotten some decent compliments about my website, so that can't be a bad thing.

Connected to the "extension of you" idea is having attractive business cards. They should be simple, in my opinion. If you live in California, you will need to show your license number on your business card. Some states require this. I know that in Washington State that is not necessary. Please do not do anything stupid like having a Rorschach card on your business card (doing so is also illegal). Just name, credentials, phone number, address, and website. There are tons of internet sites that have good templates for business cards. They make it super easy to create them, and they ship them to you. Some of the companies end up being super cheap, as well. You will need business cards, and a ton of them, so choose a design that you like. Remember that these things are also going to be an extension of you. Don't do anything that lacks class.

On Being and Staying Positive

OK, I know you have a lot to be proud of. You have weathered the storm and have completed licensure. Some of you will see your experience through a pessimistic lens. I did for a while. I thought the EPPP was way too hard and focused on the minute, unimportant deals that did not translate to a successful practice. Boy, I was right. How many times do we need to cite research that was on the EPPP? Rarely, at best. But there also was some incredibly good study information that we learned, some information that is more general, or applicable to a clinical practice.

Do not start your practice seeing through a negative lens. I know this is like starting over, and it can be completely overwhelming. I definitely agree. But, this is the start of something great. It is like starting a relationship that you know has a wealth of potential and you know is going to be lasting and fulfilling. It is going to take a tremendous amount of time and effort, but please approach these things with a positive outlook. Or do your best to fake it. You are going to have to interact with thousands of people, and first impressions matter. Sadly, people are going to view you based on their first impressions of you. So make that impression count. While most people do not have your clinical expertise, people are typically going to know if you are down or are having a bad day. They are also going to see if you are a sad, sardonic soul who views the glass as half-empty. If this is you, or if you think this is you, take a look in the mirror. Then, head to weekly therapy sessions. A pessimistic view is going to lose you money in the long run. People like being with positive people. They like referring to positive people. They don't want to refer to difficult or negative people. If this pertains to you, please give this some cognitive energy. Now this doesn't mean that you can't joke around with friends or close colleagues. This is only referring to your behavior around new people you meet or referral sources.

What I would recommend, similar to the positive psychology folks, Martin Seligman and his contemporaries, is to have a positive mindset when you are making your first contacts. When you are starting the state and government contracts, make friends, act friendly, do not treat them like dirt. This may sound obvious, but focusing on having a happy face can be tough for some. Smile when you speak to others. Yes, other people can pick up on negative nonverbal signals, too. If this is a real struggle for you, consider practicing in front of a mirror. But seriously, you are going to have a great deal of first interactions when you start your practice. Make sure that they are positive. Otherwise, it is going to cost you money and you won't be on your way to creating a financially successful clinical practice.

7

BUILDING YOUR PRIVATE PRACTICE

State and Government Work

When you first start your practice, there won't be any people coming in the door. You will go to your office and hope that the phone rings. Guess what, the phone won't ring without some hypervigilance (HVI, for those Rorschachers reading). You are going to want to consider doing some state and government work. Some colleagues look down on state and government work. But state and government work can be fantastic and meaningful. You can feel good that you are helping and improving the lives of some underserved individuals. And you can also feel good that money is continuously streaming into your bank account.

I was thinking about joining a group practice when I first started. Early in my career, when I was speaking to an older psychologist who was recruiting for her group practice, she informed me that if I wasn't on insurance panels, I "wouldn't make it." Her assertion was a pompous reminder of those who don't think outside the box. Honestly, if you are doing a ton of state and government work, you might not need to even be on insurance panels. I wasn't on the panels when I was first starting out, and I was making pretty decent money with doing the evals.

We will first discuss setting up for Social Security evaluations. Social Security disability evals are not going to go away. A good number of people are applying for Social Security at this time and they all need to be evaluated by a doctoral-level psychologist. That equates to a constant stream of work for us.

You will need to call the Social Security office and let them know that you are interested in doing cognitive and personality testing for them. Talk to them and tell them about your experience in psychological testing. They will ask for a resume and will interview you. Then you need to set up your office and then the Social Security professional relations person will come down and check out your office. The person will set you up with an account. When I got started, there was some problems with the financial office, so I didn't get paid for months . . . which was infuriating. But that process became more streamlined once my account was properly situated.

Now that we are on the topic of professional relations, I want to introduce some simple, but important, commentary about interacting with government employees. Many of the government employees that I have dealt with have been respectful to me. Please, pay respect to them. Some of them are stuck in jobs where they are dissatisfied and are doing the same things over and over again. There are some truly exceptional government employees that I have worked with, particularly my former scheduler, Linda. Linda was kind and thoughtful, and had a very high emotional IQ. She dealt with people who would likely complain to her all of the time. So I gave her compliments, I gave her positive feedback. People who get complaints all of the time, like waiters and waitresses who do fine dining, enjoy hearing good feedback too. So give good feedback and be courteous and respectful to the government workers. It doesn't matter if they don't have an advanced degree, or if they have never gone to college at all. And yes, they are going to make scheduling mistakes or other errors. But you can't blame them if the patient doesn't show up. They have to work with low-functioning individuals regularly, so be nice to them.

While you are not making $400 an hour doing government work, you can make a good living with some programs. Furthermore, you also get the chance to improve your psych testing skills. You also will be doing meaningful work that will help your community. Now this work is not without problems. I regularly get no-shows for the psych evals and the no-shows only pay $50, which really sucks. This means you are essentially getting $50 for three hours worth of work.

I started out doing psych evals for Social Security. One of my mentors, Dr. Roy Magden, told me about this program where Social Security has psychologists doing cognitive and personality assessments. I looked at the fee schedule and thought, "Man, I really don't want to do this. It doesn't pay." While no one is going to be rich doing cognitive evals for $500 a pop, remember a few things. First, these evaluations take about three hours to conduct, depending whether you are doing a WAIS, WISC, and possibly another test. The longest Social Security disability tests that I do are the WAIS and WMS combined. I typically do not do these ones as much, because the work can end up being considerably longer than four hours. But when the person is not performing well, the tests are done much more quickly. I have found that most of the time people applying for Social Security disability aren't typically IQ 130 or higher. So the bottom line is that these evaluations can be done in a relatively quick fashion. A lot of psychologists don't like doing the Social Security evaluations because the people tend to be rather low functioning. And, of course, you have the relatively high no-show rate, which screws you out of making money. But consider protecting yourself from the no-shows by finding other work to do if you encounter a no-show. For instance, if you get a no-show, you can call other patients to remind them of appointments, or work on pending psych evals. There is always something to do at the office!

Social Security disability also has other types of shorter evaluations that take about an hour to conduct—basically comprised of a clinical interview and corroborative data which you type into a report. Those pay about $180, so that is not bad for an hour or hour and one half worth of work. I can get them usually done in that amount of time because I am a seasoned typist. If you are slow with computers, it is going to take more time . . . might not even be worth it, in that case. This can be a huge money-maker, because you can do about five or six of them per day and have a $1K day. The best part is that you go home and you don't have any more work to do. Strongly consider doing these evals, as well.

When I first began writing my Social Security reports, they were about 15 pages. Now they are around 10. Why? Because they are much more streamlined and succinct. I had people at the Social Security office saying that mine were too detailed and elaborate. Now my reports are shorter, which means that they take less time. I can usually see two people for cognitive testing in a day. I see one person at 9 AM and the other at 1 PM. Now, I can't complete both reports in a day. But I do come close. In the past two years in my practice, I have probably given about 100 cognitive tests. And I'm talking complete cognitive tests, like a WAIS or WISC. Practice will help you become a quicker scorer of the results. When you become more and more familiar with the tests, you can score much of the tests as you are giving them. That ends up saving a ton of time, as well. I tend to write longer psychosocial histories, because they sometimes can provide some essential information about how the person has previously/currently been functioning. The government work is also a great opportunity to focus on your assessment skills. Since you will be doing a great deal of WAIS, WISC, and WMS evals, this is valuable experience.

So what I'm also saying is that with the government work you can make about $1K per day if you are doing it right, and if you are working hard. Chances are you, too, are a hard worker. A $1K-day is substantial. I mean, you are talking about $5K per week, and more than $200K per year. It is also more than twice what most psychologists make, according to the statistics. Not to say that you are going to make $1K per day, but that is something to strive for. As I sit here and type this, I am looking out at the ocean. Let's face it, most people adore a great view of the water. Do the government work; it doesn't pay big, but it is a smart move.

Now I am going to talk about state work. Really consider doing this when you start, because you can reap the multiple benefits right away. There are some great things that come with state work. While the money isn't always the best, similar to government work, you can meet some amazing clients and do some very meaningful work. And if you have the right approach to doing the work, the money can be pretty decent.

Some states offer state assistance programs. You can do disability evaluations for those who have mental health problems and cannot work. In Washington, this is called "General Assistance." While the money for these evaluations is not exactly going to pay for that Porsche right away, at $130 per eval, the money can add up fast. While you can achieve $1K-days doing Social Security disability evaluations, you can do this with the state, as well.

Sometimes, you will have to go into the state office to do the evaluations. This can be both good and bad, but really consider having some flexibility in this realm. Just go in there if they want you to. I also see state patients at my office, but it is nice for the state office to have people come there to be evaluated. The workers there also will appreciate that you are there doing the evals. Again, most of the employees are really nice and helpful. They appreciate what you are doing. Be courteous to them and don't act like you know everything.

Some of my colleagues do four to six state assistance evals per day. I try to do six to ten. That equals more than $1K per day, whereas they may be making half as much. This can be a HUGE discrepancy. Imagine living in a house that was half as nice. My typing skills come in really handy here, as I can complete the evals in a shorter amount of time. What is also nice is that the process for sending in the evals and sending in your billing is fairly streamlined, which means that you don't spend time on clerical stuff, which will just cost you money. The less clerical the better. I mean, come on, we didn't go to grad school to staple documents mindlessly all day long.

Working with Children

Some people don't like seeing children for therapy or assessment. Is evaluating children more difficult than evaluating adults? Sure it is. But guess what. If you don't see children you will be walking away from better economic opportunities. State and government funds usually pay a higher reimbursement rate for children. Why? Because a lot of psychologists do not want to see them. If you aren't trained in evaluating children, please read on. Otherwise, this next part may be really boring. But even if you have the proper training with evaluating children, please read on. You might be glad you did.

In most states, the government reimbursement rates are a generally higher for seeing children. For instance, in Washington, the rates are typically $100 more for a WISC-IV. Yeah, sometimes they are more work, but sometimes they are not, particularly when they fail all cognitive tasks. Many children who come through the state systems are unfortunately so low functioning that they can't manage the cognitive tasks, which is terrible news for them and their families, but it makes the evaluator's job simple. And it also happens regularly. Another good reason to see children is a thing called an independent evaluation. It is a goldmine. Why? Because you charge your rate per hour for an evaluation. Done. Make sure to get at least some of your money up front, by the way. The work can be incredibly meaningful and can also be a great balance to evaluating adults and adolescents.

Many schools need psychologists to do independent evaluations for learning disabilities or giftedness. For instance, there may be a kid who wasn't placed in the highly capable program at school. But the schools usually say that if the person wants to be in the program they can be given an independent psychological evaluation to determine if they can be in the program. Please, consider doing this work. It is fantastic work, the kids are great, and it is what cognitive testing was created for (actually, it was originally created for giftedness training, rather than evaluating mental retardation). Getting hired to do the school evaluations can be a hard process. So ask around, ask your colleagues. They might help you out. I had a colleague who had an in with a school district and he gave me the right person to call so that I was on a list of psychologists who do the independent evaluations. If you have experience doing cognitive testing for kids, this is a can't-miss opportunity, people. From a financial perspective, instead of making $600 for a government evaluation, you make $1,000. That is almost twice as much money. Let's say that you only do one government child eval per month. If you do four government evals per month or one per week for a month, you earn $2,400. Now, if you do one independent evaluation per week for a month that is $4,000. That is a TON MORE! Really consider this. If you don't you will be missing out on a great opportunity to make more money.

As mentioned earlier, roughly 1 in 88 children suffer from autistic spectrum disorders. As the world learns more about autism, there are going to be more needs for psychologists to evaluate and treat those with neurological problems. This will require extra training for psychologists, as typically neuropsychologists perform evaluations for those who suffer from autistic spectrum disorders. As these evaluations typically pay very well, I think that there will be an increasing need for neuropsychologists in the near future. For those considering internships in neuropsychology, I highly recommend that you go that route. Learning about instruments that are used to detect autism and other neurological disorders will be well worth your year internship, as gaining training in neuropsychology is a means of further differentiating yourself from other psychologists. It is a great way to make good money and do fascinating work. If you have gained training in this walk of psychology, evaluating those suffering from autistic spectrum disorders may become a lucrative portion of your private practice.

Working with Older Adults

I see a great deal of promise in the future with this work. The baby-boomers are aging and as they grow older, they will need people to provide psychological services for evaluation, assessment, and therapy. It is likely that this area will continue to grow in the next five years. I think that the older generations are viewing psychological services in a different way. In the past, going to see a psychologist was like a death march for those aged 60 and above. Seeing a psychologist today does not have the same negative stigma. And now that psychology has started to gain acceptance with older adults, there may be many more opportunities in evaluating, assessing, and treating older adults. But tread carefully here, as the best financial opportunities likely lie with cash opportunities.

I was fortunate enough to take a class on psychological services with older adults when I was in graduate school. If you have not done this, I highly recommend it. Learning about assessing and treating older adults is fascinating, particularly as science teaches us more about the brain. There will be more and more of a need to perform different evaluations for older adults, such as Alzheimer's evaluations and evaluating other forms of dementia. Unfortunately for many clinical psychologists, the training necessary for such evaluations involves neuropsychological work that you learn through predoc years or postdoc placements. I do not have a great deal of experience evaluating Alzheimer's disease, since I did not do a neurological placement for internships or postdocs. If you are interested in this field, you might want to consider doing a neuropsych postdoc. These postdocs are also highly competitive, so you will need to do well during your predoc years to gain such a postdoc. My colleague Dr. Renee Low was able to gain a postdoc at UC Davis and has learned a great deal about these evaluations.

While I have training in assessing memory and executive functioning, I do not have a background doing Alzheimer's assessments. Typically, neuropsychological evaluations can help better understand the nature of the cognitive/memory impairment, as well as the individual's cognitive/memory strengths and weaknesses. The numbers are staggering: 5.4 million Americans are currently living with Alzheimer's disease. Roughly 16 percent of women and 11 percent of men over age 71 have Alzheimer's disease. Nearly 50 percent of adults over 85 have Alzheimer's disease. Alzheimer's is the sixth leading cause of death in the United States. The direct cost of caring for those with Alzheimer's disease is around $200 billion, including $140 billion to Medicare and Medicaid. Now I want to warn you that doing Alzheimer's evaluations is not a good reason to become a Medicare provider. As noted earlier, you do not want to be a Medicare provider if you want to run a financially successful private practice, as reimbursement with Medicare are some of the worst out there, if not the worst. You may find that some families will want you to do evaluations that are cash based. While I have not found this to be particularly true, some individuals will want to have formal memory or cognitive testing done, and this may be a good opportunity for clinicians in the future. In this case, it is best to only accept good providers or to accept cash for your evaluations. The latter may be very rare, as relatively few individuals and family can pay cash for evaluations. This will also depend on the area that you are practicing, as more people are likely to pay cash in Beverly Hills, California, than in Fairbanks, Alaska.

Psychotherapy also has its opportunity, as long as you do not use Medicare as a provider. Some older adults shift over to Medicare for their health care services, which won't help your private practice become financially successful. However, I have found that some older individuals prefer to use cash when paying for their appointments. And then there are other individuals who prefer to use traditional insurance companies, such as Aetna, for their psychological services. Serving older adults is meaningful work, but be careful what insurance carriers you use for providing care. It may be possible for you to provide group therapy for those suffering from Alzheimer's disease and also for families of those suffering from Alzheimer's disease or other forms of dementia. Group therapy, particularly on a cash basis, is a good way to make money. For instance, if you charge $40 per person, per session, and you have eight people in the group, you pocket $320, which is incredible money. That number goes down to $160 if you charge $20 per head. But particularly if you have experience running groups at a predoc or postdoc level, you might want to consider starting a group. While my practice is full and I do not currently have time to run groups, I have long considered going this route.

Depression in the elderly is a major epidemic. In fact, the National Alliance on Mental Health (NAMI) indicates that 6.5 million of the 35 million adults aged 65 and older suffer from depression. Older women are also twice as likely to be depressed as older men. So it is likely that you will be seeing an older woman in the office, rather than an older man. Again, group therapy for women struggling with depression may be a great opportunity here, particularly if you have experience running groups. There may also be opportunities for independent evaluations for depression, but generally I have not found that to be the case. If you are not doing group therapy, you might find that performing non-Medicare evaluations for older adults is a better way to be financially successful, since many older adults needing psychotherapy will likely want to use Medicare. These are all important things to consider when working with older adults.

Independent Evaluations

Sometimes I am asked to do independent evaluations. These can be for a variety of referral questions. For instance, a lawyer might want me to evaluate someone who has suffered some trauma to determine if they are suffering from PTSD. Or a parent might want me to do a giftedness assessment for their 4th-grade son. The bottom line is that these independent evaluations can be a goldmine for psychologists. You have to be careful about lawyers, because some of them want the outcome that suits them. You need to be paid for the hours work and it is your clinical judgment. Sometimes, the lawyers will choose not to take the report if it doesn't suit them.

When you get a referral for an independent eval, you will be in the rare situation where you choose your rate. I recommend that you choose a rate that is not on the low side but on the high side. Now I know that we aren't supposed to talk about what we charge as psychologists, and I'm not going to break any rules here. But don't charge a low hourly rate for these evals. There is something to be said about having a higher rate. People respect you more if your rate is on the higher side. At the same time, you don't want to charge such a high rate that you will never get referrals again.

Sometimes people might ask you to lower your rate. For instance, I have had lawyers ask me before to lower my rate for evaluation. First, my rate is not ridiculous by any means. Second, the lawyers are undoubtedly CHARGING A CONSIDERABLY HIGHER HOURLY RATE THAN I DO! We need to protect our profession here. Don't buckle with these kinds of things. At times, you might get a referral from an individual who does not have the money for your full rate. In this case, it is OK to lower your rate, in compliance with APA ethics code standards. I would not recommend that you do this regularly if you want to be financially successful, but some people are not going to be able to afford your standard hourly rate, and we have an ethical responsibility to try to provide services for those who do not have the means to receive services. I recommend that you do occasional sliding-scale evaluations or pro-bono evaluations. It can be very meaningful work.

Sometimes, you will have to also explain the benefits of a psychological evaluation. Just try to explain as honestly as you can. Don't sugarcoat anything and don't say anything like, "I think it looks good for this person." Lawyers will ask you if you think that the person should be evaluated and whether the results will look good. Just tell them that you don't know. Honestly, how can you know unless you have the test results? You don't. What I do is tell them that the results may be good and they may be bad . . . and that I have absolutely no way of knowing without analyzing the test data.

Lawyers have also told me that "there is nothing wrong with this person, please evaluate them." Well, while they may be right, just explain that you don't know anything until you do the psychological testing. Trust me, some of them work hard to try to sway you. They will say the results should be in the client's favor. Well, how would they know, unless they have the background in psychology? Do they have a great clinical inference? Don't be influenced in the least bit. Just do your job and you will do fine.

Sometimes, I am asked to perform evaluations for personal injury cases. The lawyer will call me to find out whether the client is suffering from depression, anxiety, PTSD, or other psychological problems. Again, in this case it is imperative that you focus on the test data, just in case you are called into court. There is more of a focus on evidence-based practice in psychology today. The more you can focus on your test data and the less you can rely on clinical judgment, the better your results will hold up in court.

I also recommend that you do a thorough job when you are asked to do these evaluations. Please, don't cut corners with the evaluations. Also, remember that your reputation is at stake here. Make sure to dot all your I's and cross all of your T's. Don't have any typos in your evals. I have done that before and it is just embarrassing. Now, I know, if you are doing a 30-page psych eval, there may be one or two imperfections. But really try to do a good job. I've gotten teased by a lawyer in court for having the wrong pronoun in a document. And it was embarrassing. The fact that they teased me for one typo in a 30-page document is completely ridiculous. Then again, it is something that I shouldn't have done. Aspire to perfection here. Hire an editor if you need to. Make sure to use the most clinically validated tests. I am talking about the WAIS IV, MMPI-2, etc. Don't give tests that are not well known or do not have high reliability and validity. This is just part of doing a good job and doing high-quality work. If you don't do this, you may not get the referrals again. That can mean the difference between $0–10K or more per year (depending on how many you do).

Medicaid/Medicare

Whether or not to sign up for Medicare or not is a real issue of contention for a lot of psychologists. This is a hard, multifaceted issue. I want you to really think about what you are getting into. I think a lot of psychologists who are starting out don't know what these programs are about. So they sign up and then they have a ton of clients who are on these programs. There are some good things about Medicare/Medicaid. I mean, the system appears to be minimally intrusive—meaning that you really only have to offer minimal documentation, such as diagnosis, treatment codes, etc. The same is not true for dealing with work-injured patients, who require a good deal of patient notes, constant contact with claims managers, etc. However, Medicare/Medicaid is not a good way to create a financially successful private practice in clinical psychology, while the clinical hours with work-injured patients is. Medicare therapy doesn't pay, and the evaluations don't pay. I am going to go out on a limb here and offer a resounding "don't do this!" Who knows what it is going to be like in the future when you won't be able to terminate your contract and you will have to continue to see these patients even though they don't pay well. Really do your research here.

One thing that you should know if you are starting a practice is that the reimbursement rates for Medicare/Medicaid tend to be much lower than the rates for other good insurance carriers. They also can be more complicated to deal with. Another major downside from having a Medicare/Medicaid contract is that you can't terminate your contract. You are stuck with the contract and you have to see the patients, except in very rare circumstances. The APA in 2010 indicated that roughly 40 percent of clinical psychologists in private practice do not accept Medicare and 55 percent do not accept Medicaid. Many psychologists opt out of Medicare and Medicaid. According to the APA survey in 2010, the major reason why psychologists did not accept either carrier was the low reimbursement rates. Now this can cause a problem with older people receiving psychological treatment. Of course, this is a social problem. But remember, this book is not about social problems. I could write a whole other book on social problems. This is about helping you make money as a psychologist. It is about giving you financial freedom that you didn't think you would have. Remember, you are in the driver's seat here. Don't do Medicare/Medicaid unless you have to. That is my best advice. My advice also includes having a lawyer look over your Medicare/Medicaid contract, because there is some very interesting language written into the contract. I had my lawyer peruse the document. And after finding out that I can't leave the contract as long as I am licensed, I decided to "leave" the plan altogether. Please do the research with this one, my friends. I would be much more comfortable with you doing state and government psych evals than doing Medicare work. The bottom line is that if you work hard, you are going to make a ton more money doing state and government work.

Working with State and Government Employees

If you are going to be doing state and government work, you are going to be working with the respective employees. For instance, I see state employees every week, doing general assistance evaluations. I think part of the reason why I got in right away with doing state work is because I was able to connect with the state workers. Some of these people do not enjoy their jobs and are underpaid and underworked. You will meet people like Vu, a 60-year old Vietnamese-American who has been working as a state social worker for 30 years. Vu is relatively difficult to understand, as he speaks with a heavy accent. He took a few months to get to know, as he would generally give very short answers. But I got to know him, his background, his family, and his hobbies. And I found that under the shell was a kind, intelligent, and gentle-hearted man who loves to help people. Another employee, Matt, prides himself on being caustic and difficult. He also wants you to talk back to him and wants you to challenge him. Remember that working with employees is something that can be a wonderful thing, as there are all types of state workers, just as there are all types of people who you will be evaluating. Take Michael, a younger Vietnamese-American family man. Like Vu, Michael took some time getting to know, as he was very shy and reticent for the first few months that I was going into the state office. But after some time, he gained trust and saw me as someone with whom he can chat with or discuss cases. We have a nice working relationship. He wants to help me and I want to help him. He fills in my no-shows and I do the reports in a timely fashion. As an aside, never turn down seeing someone, regardless of their level of psychopathology. He knows I work hard, and he respects me, and I respect him.

Use your clinical inference with the employees just as you would with therapy patients. Use empathy when necessary. Be respectful and courteous, and you will do great. One thing also to remember is that some of these people dislike their jobs. Their work can be very high stress. Don't give them any attitude, because they have been getting attitude 24/7 by the people they see. I know that you are the doctor going in there. But don't be disrespectful about it. If they want you to come in and do psych evals, they already know that you are cool.

Sometimes, while working for the state, they will ask you to come into the office, while in other cases you will be able to see the people at your office. Both are good experiences. Remember that some of the people coming to your office may be homeless, so they may struggle with self-care. Personally, I have found that the lower-functioning clients are more courteous and respectful when they come to my office, rather than when they are seen at the state office. Pretty much none of the clientele enjoys being at the state office to begin with. Many of the state offices in Washington State are located in sterile, archaic buildings. The waiting areas are usually malodorous and crammed full of people. Particularly for those suffering from anxiety disorders, sitting and waiting at the state office is not a good experience. Many people have admitted that they prefer coming to my office, where it is clean, well kept, and relatively spacious. Definitely one downside of doing the state work is that there tends to be an aura of cigarette smoke that can infiltrate your office. Many of the individuals whom I evaluate are heavy smokers and so I end up spraying the office regularly, and I also have a window that I can open to cope with the smell. I am not trying to be condescending here; I just want to paint as realistic picture as I can. If you can't handle the smell of cigarette smoke/body odor and if you don't have a window in your office that you can open, you likely will not want to do this kind of work. I mean, this just makes sense, because many of the people are homeless or do not have adequate self-care.

Working with low-functioning people may test your ego strength. Some people will try to anger you, as they have followed this pattern of behavior for many years. Don't fall into the trap. If you have experience with working with lower-functioning people, fall back on your previous experiences and training. Listen attentively and they will see that they can trust you with information. If you are present with them, this will help you immensely. I have even had people whom I am evaluating start yelling at me from the beginning of the clinical interview. I've been called every name in the book for asking simple questions about a person's history. There may be some safety issues with working with these individuals, as I have a female colleague who was nearly assaulted while doing Social Security disability evaluations. You may want to consider having pepper spray in your desk, just in case someone is acutely psychotic or is having homicidal ideation. If you are not comfortable, don't enter a domain where you aren't comfortable. Use your best clinical judgment when working with low-functioning individuals. Don't fall for any traps. People might tell you that you don't know anything. Just continue the evaluation and be nonchalant about the insult. They are trying to get you, just as they try to get everyone. If you don't want to work with lower-functioning individuals, don't do state-funded work. But working and helping these people can be incredibly rewarding, even if it can be taxing at times. Not everyone who comes through the state office door is low functioning. Many people that I have evaluated are successful men and women who have fallen on hard times.

A wonderful part of doing state work is that many of the people really need immediate help. In Washington State, people can be placed on the general assistance program for periods of up to one year. Sometimes, they are on the program even longer, although I think recent legislation has been trying to change that. Either way, the program is fantastic for those who simply cannot work because of their mental health problems. Just as a welder cannot work with a broken right arm, many people cannot work, even on a part-time basis, because of major mental health problems. Evaluating people on state assistance allows me, as a clinician, to see a ton of different people. I am literally seeing all spectrums of the DSM-IV. This is a tremendous experience to see so many different diagnoses, and a great chance to improve my diagnostician skills. So the benefits of state work are clear. Do state work and earn a decent living (provided that you do a lot of evals) and become a better clinician. Seems like a pretty easy choice to me.

Now there is another issue with seeing clients who are lower functioning—they tend to have higher no-show rates. People no-show their appointments for myriad reasons. The bottom line is when a client no-shows, that negatively impacts your bottom line. I am not going to say that there is a great way to prevent no-shows from happening. One thing you can do is call the client before the appointment, if possible, and if you have their number. For some evaluations that you do with the state and government, you might not have their phone number. I have had clients who were seen for Social Security who did not show up to their appointments, and then when I called them, they ended up coming in. Miracles like this actually do happen sometimes. But some of the people are in dire straits and they might miss their appointment because of homelessness, abuse, divorce, delinquency, drugs, you name it. With those, there will be nothing that you can do to prevent no-shows. Another issue is that when your practice starts getting full, you won't have time to offer reminder calls to people. And sometimes you will call and you will get their voicemails, answering services or, in some cases, the number will be disconnected. That is always a fun one. So I'll offer the bottom line with this one. If you have time, call the patient ahead of time. If you don't and if they miss their appointment, try to get them in or at least reschedule them (if you are allowed to do so).

How does the no-show affect your bottom line? Well, there can be some grave financial implications for no-shows. For instance, a psych eval for the government usually is around $500. Well, their no-show rate in Washington is $50. Let's say that you are doing one government eval per week. That would mean $2K per month if everyone shows up. Now, if nobody shows up, that means you would be losing $1,800 per month. Per year, that means $19K. That is a hell of a lot of money. You can't always predict no-shows. Sometimes they come in masses. But they are like the plague to having a financially successful private practice in psychology. Do your best to prevent them and if they do happen, do your best to get them in your office ASAP, if possible.

Vocational Rehabilitation

Another opportunity through the state is doing vocational reha-bilitation evaluations. You can find them online, as they have offices throughout your state. In California, the program is called Department of Rehabilitation, while in Washington it is called Department of Vocational Rehabilitation. Either way, most states have this program. The programs were instated to provide resources for job seekers with disabilities. Some disabilities may be physical and others may be cognitive/mental health. These evaluations provide the clinician with some excellent opportunities to improve psychological testing skills in both cognitive and personality domains.

To start doing these evaluations, you will need to be on the panel for the region. Each state has different regions. For instance, when I was in graduate school in San Diego, the region was San Diego County. You should apply with the region where you are interested in working. Go into the office and talk to the supervisor there, who will be able to guide you to the correct person. They will want a copy of your resume and will likely want to talk about your experience doing psych evals. If you have experience doing both cognitive and personality testing, talk about your experiences. If you have ever worked with rehabilitation clients, let them know. They may tell you that they already have psychologists that they refer to, but they might say that you are eligible to be on a panel. Another idea is to talk to individual rehabilitation counselors, and see if they are interested in referring to you. It never hurts to talk to them about your experience. When you are talking to the people at the rehabilitation office, try not to tout yourself too much. If you have applicable experience, let them know, but don't say that you are an expert or that you know everything. They won't appreciate that. Don't be afraid to talk about experiences, but don't discuss all of your accolades. Exercise some humility.

I have done vocational evaluations in both Washington and California, and I really enjoy that the counselors working with the evaluation subjects are usually helpful and insightful. Typically, they also give you excellent and thoughtful referral questions. You will need to think about the following questions: What kind of work can these people do? What are the client's cognitive limitations, and (based on their personality) where would he or she be best suited to land a job? Some of the people are high school dropouts who aspire to be a medical doctor. Not that it is bad to dream, but some of their goals may be aspirational rather than realistic. So you will get a referral question such as, "What kind of work can this person do based on their personality and cognitive ability?" And then you will tailor your psych testing based on the question. When doing these evals, I typically lean towards the best, most well-researched instruments, such as the MMPI, WAIS, etc. I highly recommend you to do the same, just in case you go to court and they ask you why you didn't use the best-researched instrument. The people working at Department of Rehabilitation are great, too. Take Eric, a vocational counselor who has been in the field for more than 20 years. Eric is very savvy with clients and can be caustic at times. He is a hilarious man who commutes about one hour each way to work and loves his job. He is one of the many great people who work for this branch and really wants to help others find a job. That's their altruistic gig.

Now I will discuss the money aspect. These evaluations can be time consuming and do not pay well. But the people you are evaluating usually do not have major Axis II personality psychopathology, and they are typically some of the most interesting people that I evaluate. Some of them have been working for many years, suffered a setback and are desperate to get back to work. It is great evaluating these types of people. And with vocational evaluations, there are all types of referral questions. The work is both challenging and rewarding. The pay is substandard but it still will pay the bills. Typically I get about $600 per evaluation, which ends up being less than $100 an hour. Not great. But do these things, anyway. While the financial gain is not great, it is still money in the bank and the evaluations are never a headache. And you never know when a good evaluation contact will lead to a recommendation or referral.

Other State Evaluations

Depending on the state, there are other opportunities to perform psychological evaluations. For instance, you may be able to do evaluations for the elderly or for those who have disabilities. Each state is different, so I recommend calling each office and seeing if psychologists do evaluations for their department. Offer to send them a copy of your resume . . . don't be shy here. Talk to your colleagues about other departments that are available for psychologists. Your colleagues will know which ones pay better and which ones are available. I would also recommend contacting your state psychological association to get more information about state work opportunities for psychologists.

Mental Health Screening Evaluations for Medical Purposes

This subject has recently been a new area of opportunity for psychologists, as medical doctors are requiring psychological evaluations for patients wanting to have various procedures performed, such as lap-band surgery, gastric bypass surgery, and plastic surgery. I have been contacted by various medical doctors to do psych evals for those who are going to have a spinal stimulator procedure.

To get in with the medical specialists, you will need to know medical doctors in the area. I suggest talking to them about those who do the screening procedures and then asking the specialists out to dinner or lunch. It never hurts to drop by their office, brings some cards, and ask if they have a few minutes of their time. It is probably best to call them first, though, in case they are not in the office or are too busy for a short meeting. Most of the medical specialists will want to talk to you so that you can be a credible referral source. Consider bringing a resume and many business cards. Dress nicely and conservatively.

These screening evaluations are usually short and do not require a ton of psychological testing. Depending on the referral question and what the medical doctor wants, you usually just conduct a clinical history with a thorough psychosocial history and then include an objective testing measure, like the MMPI-2. Usually, these evaluations pay well for psychologists, as the insurance companies may or may not pay for the evaluations, so the patient will need to pay out of pocket for the evaluation. If you are being paid by insurance, be advised that they may fight about payment. These parameters may depend on the state. While these evaluations have been a recent trend in psychological testing, I have a distinct feeling that this area will continue to grow. More and more Americans want to have the lap-band surgery or plastic surgery performed. I do not expect this trend to decrease in the near future.

These evaluations are a good idea, because you do not want people with major psychological issues having these potentially serious medical procedures conducted. Insurance companies are also worried about being sued, so some of them are paying for the evaluations. I think there is a trend toward having psychologists perform these evaluations because the medical doctors are concerned that they will be sued by a patient with major psychological problems. These evaluations are a good way to make money, and they also have the added benefit of allowing you to work with individuals who usually do not have serious issues. You are typically not going to find very low-functioning individuals in these evaluations, which makes your job easier. Also, many of the evaluations are not through insurance and are cash based, which will help your bottom line even more. I have found that those needing the medical procedures are some great people who generally do not have major psychological issues. Some of them will be surprised that a psychological evaluation is necessary, so you will need to explain to them about what you will be doing and how it is just a standard procedure for everyone needing the surgery. This will make them feel more comfortable and will help create rapport.

Custody Evaluations

This section is for the adrenaline seekers. I was fortunate enough to have some predoctoral experience with child custody evaluations. The experience afforded me the opportunity to do some child custody work once I was establishing my private practice. Now, I want to warn you that child custody work is not for everyone. But the work can be lucrative, if you have the right business plan. It can be also incredibly meaningful work.

The state of Washington. where I practice, pays for child custody evaluations, where you evaluate the parents and determine their mental health issues and issues that may affect their parenting abilities. This is very high-stress work, because some of the people who are being evaluated are having marked mental health issues, yet contend that they are good parents. While the clientele varies greatly, I would not recommend doing this kind of work unless you have some predoctoral experience with evaluating parents for custody. You might also find that after you complete the evaluations, the parents may continually call you or harass you (which happened to me). Financially speaking, the pay rates vary from state to state. The best financial gain for you comes with doing court testimony with these cases, as you are able to charge your own rate and the court will pay your rate. At this current juncture in my career, I have found this work to be too stressful for the amount of reimbursement that it offers. While I find the work particularly meaningful and intellectually challenging, I have scaled back with child custody evaluations, as I have found interest in other walks of a clinical practice. I think that starting your practice with child custody work is one of the riskier ways to begin your practice. Without clinical training or experience doing these evaluations, I would strongly recommend that you choose to do other evaluations, such as Social Security evaluations or other independent evaluations. Doing child custody evaluations puts you at one of the highest risks for litigation against psychologists. Pickar has noted the importance of maintaining the forensic role during these evaluations, which is, of course, very different from maintaining a therapeutic role. Pickar (2007) also maintains the importance of overcoming biases, as well as countertransferential issues in your role as an evaluator, as many parents undergoing child custody evaluations project anger and frustration onto the evaluator. It is clear that if you struggle with these issues as a clinician, you are best advised against doing child custody. It should be noted that child custody evaluations yield the second-most numerous ethics complaints to the APA, only behind sexual misconduct (APA, 2002), so undertaking child custody evaluations are one of the more risky choices for clinical work. I highly recommend purchasing Bartol and Bartol's work *Introduction to Forensic Psychology*, which provides an abundance of helpful information about forensic evaluation, consulting with the court, and criminal psychology work.

On Giving Testimony

I had the rare opportunity to befriend a few attorneys when I moved from California to Washington. Joining some local organizations, such as the Young Professionals organization, gave me the opportunity to meet people from a variety of different professions. As I got acquainted with some area lawyers, I knew that in order for me to improve as an expert witness, I should be trained by lawyers to learn more about what I might expect as an expert witness. I learned a great deal through area lawyers about what questions lawyers might ask, and how I should best field the questions. I also learned and read the books given to lawyers about cross-examining psychologists, so I have a better understanding about what questions they might ask. I would recommend paying for at least five hours of practice with a lawyer when you are doing forensic work, and also choose a lawyer who will help you along and will not undermine your learning. I chose two area lawyers with whom I regularly consult regarding family law cases. I have a good relationship with them and have learned a great deal about family law from them. My relationship with them further illustrates the importance of getting to know other professionals in your community by joining local organizations (such as Young Professionals or the Rotary Club). The more meaningful professional contacts you have, the more financially successful you will be as a private practice psychologist.

I had some predoctoral experience in learning about forensic psychology, as a few of my clinical supervisors had extensive experience in this realm. Learning from them also was a key in knowing how to defend my psych evals. I also learned a great deal from a mentor, Dr. Roy Magden, a psychologist from the Tacoma, Washington, area. When I moved back to Washington, over various lunches and coffees, I learned more about his experience in forensic psychology. Dr. Magden is someone I greatly admire. Trained by Rogers and also Ellis (strangely enough), Dr. Magden also graduated from California School of Professional Psychology, San Diego, and has been doing forensic psychology work for more than 30 years. In fact, he taught me just as much about child custody evaluations as I had learned in my predoctoral training. He told me keys to being a successful expert witness, such as knowing the reliability and validity of the instruments used, memorizing the important research connected with the instruments used, and applying the research to the cases. So, my point here is to try to find a mentor, if possible. It is not only important to learn from lawyers, but also to find a mentor who has many years of experience with giving expert witness testimony. Finally, do the research on the instruments. If you are doing expert testimony on a patient diagnosed with PTSD, explain the research with various instruments that measure PTSD, such as the MMPI-2, the TSI and how the instruments effectively can serve as a diagnostic tool. If you do the research, you will give successful testimony.

Practice giving testimony. If needed, practice in front of the mirror, in front of your boyfriend/girlfriend, in front of friends, but practice until you are competent. Never go into testimony without knowing the research on the instruments or the research on the diagnoses that you gave. Know the diagnoses in and out and how they differentiate from other diagnoses. It is essential to review the DSM-IV TR, as well as the latest edition, the DSM-V. A savvy lawyer will know both the DSM-IV TR and the DSM-V, and will ask you about the different diagnoses. So, being a good diagnostician is paramount. You need to know the type of language to use in the courts. For instance, it is important for you to use psychological language that others can understand. Using certain psychological terms, such as anhedonia , may not be appropriate. Consistency in your content and language is key.

Consult regularly with other psychologists who give expert testimony. It never hurts to put a call into a colleague when you have a question about a diagnosis or if you think that they might know more than you about a specific psychological instrument. For instance, I have a colleague who knows a great deal about the psychopath personality (as well as antisocial personality disorder). This is not my area of expertise and it is also somewhat clinically rare to see such a condition. But when I have a question about the disorder, I give Dr. Kropp a call. So know your colleagues and what their specific area of expertise is—and don't be afraid to call them whenever you have questions. Most good colleagues will call you back if you have a clinical question. Giving testimony can be financially lucrative. In most courts, you can charge your hourly rate for expert witness rate. While I wouldn't recommend charging more than $500 per hour for this work, don't low-ball yourself, either. Remember that some medical doctors charge somewhere around $1K per hour (hard to believe, huh?) for their expert work, so don't undermine your value as a professional.

Insurance Panels

When you get your practice started, you will need to apply to be on insurance panels. Many psychologists do therapy, but are not skilled in testing, which is why it is good to have a background in psychological testing. Insurance panels will like that you do psych testing, that you see children and adolescents. They will not like it if you only do therapy for adults. Most people do that, and the panels won't see you as a big asset to them. Don't have the attitude that you won't ever need to be on the panels either because you probably will need to be on at least a couple of them. They provide steady referrals, and while insurance doesn't always pay very well, there are definitely some that pay better than others. Some people think that when you start, you don't have to be on insurance panels to be financially successful. I would say that this is very rarely true. In most cases, if you aren't on insurance panels, you aren't going to be getting enough referrals to meet your financial goals. Very few people are going to be financially successful when they start out by only seeing private paying patients. While it is not a ton of fun applying and there can be up to many months of waiting to be approved for the panel, I want to try to explain that there is a right way to go through this process. And not all insurance panels are the same.

To apply, you need to go to the insurance company's respective websites and you will have applications to fill out. Most of them will just have you check boxes or write little blurbs about your experience, as there will likely be no extensive essays or anything too daunting. The applications do usually take an hour or more to fill out and I found that a portion of the application is not applicable to psychologists. When you are filling them out, do not be shy about your background or experience. If you have training in EMDR, list it. If you speak Spanish, definitely list it. The insurance panel is looking for someone who is going to be a tangible asset to them. If you only do therapy for adults, that is not much of an asset, because most everyone else does that as well. But if you do therapy for children as well as adults, that is going to be a much greater asset for them. They also want people who have experience with psychological testing, and if you will do psychological testing for children and adolescents, that is an added bonus.

You may run into the unfortunate predicament of having an insurance panel be closed to applicants because they already have plenty of psychologists. That's what happened to me when I first joined Regence/ Blue Shield. The panel for psychologists was closed and they weren't accepting new applicants. The reason why I ended up getting on there was my persistence and also the fact that I see a variety of people for a variety of services. They liked that and eventually added me. It is best to be persistent with the insurance companies to let them know that you can be an asset to them. Explain your experience, your clinical areas of expertise, and why your services are needed in your community. It is sad that we must do this, but the insurance companies really don't care whether you get on or not. They are huge businesses focused on making money. Insurance companies are highly profitable and have very strong lobbying positions at both the state and federal levels.

Many of the insurance panels don't accept new psychologists and ask that you be licensed one (or more) years before you can get on their panel. I have found that it is usually the best ones that don't accept new psychologists. At least in the Washington area, this is the case. Some of my other colleagues mention that predicament to be true in Southern California, as well. That is why you have state and government contracts beforehand, so that you don't get stuck in this dilemma. Some of this depends on where you are living, as it is typically easier to get on the best panels if you are living in more rural locations.

Look into which panels are better than others. Talk to your colleagues about this. I had some very blunt conversations with older psychologists about which panels were good, which were bad, and why you should be on one rather than the other. I am on a few panels but am not on all of the carriers. I found out which ones were the best for psychologists, which ones were minimally intrusive for the patients, and which ones reimbursed the best (hey, this book IS about money, after all). So far so good. I am seeing plenty of people on insurance, including work-injured patients, through the state insurance. Really do the research on what panels are good and what ones don't have the best reputation.

Consider talking to your state organization about this. Consult with experienced psychologists about this. I don't care if you have to pay them, this will be money well spent.

There can be huge differences in reimbursement rates. Imagine if you were seeing patients for $130 per hour rather than seeing them for a $100 reimbursement rate. That is almost 30 percent more money in your pocket. There is a huge difference in 30 percent. That's the difference between $70K and $100K. Don't choose the panels that pay poorly. I don't care if you are just starting out, don't do it.

Look into the panels contracts, as well. Some of them may disallow you from getting off them. Medicare/Medicaid does that. You may want to consider having an attorney review the insurance panel contract with you. Filling out those contracts are time-consuming and nothing short of an utter pain. Set aside time to do them and make sure to fill them out accurately and completely.

A Cash Practice

I have some colleagues who have established cash practices by not being on insurance panels. I can remember that when I was in graduate school, I aspired to having a cash practice because some of my graduate school professors admitted that they had cash-only practices. I soon found out that when you start your private practice, having a cash-only practice can be very difficult. And not only from my experience, but also from consulting with other colleagues, I have found that a cash-only practice is not the best way to make a lot of money when you are setting up your practice. Let me explain.

A major reason not to do this is because medical doctors and other referral sources, such as specialists who give you referrals, are typically seeing insurance patients, rather than cash patients. Lawyers also might give you referrals for therapy and most of those will be insurance patients. Some medical doctors and other referral sources might see you as elitist if you are only taking cash, which is typically not the best way to gain rapport with your referral source. There are only a few people out there who are willing to pay cash for your services. They typically live in affluent areas, so if you want to set up this type of practice, be prepared to have higher overheads—which is a further reason why having a cash-based practice is not the best idea. And in more affluent areas, surely some people are going to be willing to pay cash rather than use insurance. But this is not the way to go if you want to be financially successful. Let's say that you are seeing 20 people per week, all insurance people, and you are doing a few state and government cognitive or personality evals, as well. Let's say that you make $2.5k per week from insurance reimbursements from those therapy patients, and you make another $1K per week on the state and government evals. That's $3.5K per week. Now compare this to seeing only cash patients. Maybe you charge $140 per hour. That means that you are going to have to see 25 cash patients for therapy that week. Let's say that you also see one cash psych eval (which are typically rare) for $1K. That still means that you are going to have to see 18 cash patients for therapy that week. It is going to be really difficult for you to get that many cash patients for therapy. I am going to say that it is nearly impossible to accomplish that goal, unless you have a very established practice—one where you have been actively networking and have been bringing in referrals for many years. My point is that setting up a cash-only practice seems like a good idea. And you might just have those lofty aspirations of a cash practice in undergrad or grad school. But having a cash practice is clearly not the best way to make money when you are starting your private practice in psychology.

Work-Injured Patients

The assessment and treatment of work-injured patients has been some of the most rewarding work that I have encountered in clinical psychology. Before we talk money, think about this . . . what a tremendous opportunity it is to help someone who is work-injured, cannot work, and has suffered mental health problems, and then you help them and they are able to return to work. Talk about rewarding. You have helped restore someone's livelihood. This is just as important as helping someone be a better parent. I mean, you are talking about inherent survival here. People need to work in order to live. You are helping people be better able to survive. We are getting very high on the hierarchy of needs here.

If you decide to see work-injured patients, you are going to get all types. You will see blue-collar workers, white-collar workers, in literally all types of vocations. And if nothing else, how great is it to be able to see someone who is highly educated and someone who is not. You will see individuals engaged in completely different occupations who are suffering from very similar problems. You will also get some tremendous differences in age ranges. For instance, I have seen a 19-year-old woman one hour and then the next I have seen a 70-year-old man.

I have found that with work-injured patients you tend to see a ton of depression, anxiety, somatic problems, and insomnia. These are very compelling issues. And the insomnia component further complicates mental health problems. Anyone who cannot sleep a wink is going to have some grave mental health issues (with very few exceptions). Most of these issues are completely treatable, which is also fantastic. In rare cases, you will see some Axis II personality psychopathology that has been worsened by the work injury. That becomes more complicated. Sometimes when evaluating these people, I indicate that they are not the best fit for my clinical practice. I do not have a wealth of experience with therapeutic interventions for those diagnosed with personality disorders, so I typically send them to someone else, except for some rare cases. I have actually found that Axis II in work-injured patients tends to be pretty rare. And this makes sense . . . many of those who suffer from grave Axis II psychopathology can't work well and are usually fired or quit. That is different from these people who have been working well and are injured on the job. Many work-injured patients also suffer marital or relationship issues due to the work injury. And this just makes sense, as they have previously been working well and providing/contributing for their families, and then that stops and there are big changes. Usually that leads to financial troubles. Sometimes, there are major adjustment issues with someone being at home all day when they were previously working. Working through these adjustment issues and moving forwards by creating future goals can be one of the many wonderful aspects of working with work-injured patients.

Now we come to the financial component. Please see work-injured patients when you are starting your practice, because it pays. Yes, the reimbursement rates tend to be much higher than other insurance companies. While dealing with this realm can be a logistical and administrative nightmare, it is well worth it if you have a competent biller. And mine is more than competent. She has been in the game for a long time. Do your best to get work-injured patients in your office and try to make reminder calls when you can, because when you work with work-injured patients, if you don't see them, you can't bill for them. In Washington, there are no no-show fees for patients who miss their appointments. So you need to do your best to remind them of their appointments. I always give them a card with their appointment time and when I can, I give them reminder calls of their appointments. This will greatly help you with getting them consistently to their appointments. Now for that bad part . . .

Why is seeing work-injured patients an administrative nightmare? Well, there have been times when I haven't been paid for four months worth of work. I am serious, four months. When you get paid, it is a handsome reward. Want to hear about more problems? How about this: inept claims managers. I have had Bachelor's-level claims managers who have told me that I was wrong with my evaluation and I didn't know what I was talking about. Talk about some serious Axis II! Dealing with the claims managers can be a real problem when working with work-injured patients. And I have myriad stories where the claims managers have been difficult/rude/narcissistic. You will have to deal with them because they are the ones who approve treatment for the patients. They have a power position and many of them get off on telling people what to do. There are definitely some plusses and minuses with this area. But I would argue that the plusses, both financial and professional, outweigh the minuses, usually with the administrative work. Sometimes, I will have my bookkeeper call the claims managers when I don't have time or when I am frustrated. I'll remind you again that you need to find some good people on your team. They will help you out and literally do things that you (and literally everyone else) don't want to do. I even hired a person who works on delinquent accounts with the state, and she does a good job working with difficult claims managers.

While therapy and assessment of work-injured patients have higher reimbursement rates, I have also had terrible things happen, like the claims manager does not enter the right code for therapy and then I don't get paid for months because of their negligence. This is the kind of thing that happens regularly. It will likely happen to you and you will just have to deal with constant frustrating issues. My experience, and that of my colleagues, indicate that if you complain about insurance companies' negligence, usually nothing happens, and it is typically a waste of your time.

Some of the work-injured patients that I treat speak Spanish. Since I do not speak Spanish, an interpreter is present at each therapy sessions. The presence of an interpreter can induce some issues with the people I am treating/evaluating. I have found that it is particularly difficult to give any mental status examinations to those who speak Spanish. It is very difficult to do any immediate memory recall tasks because of the interpreter's lack of background in psychological testing. Sometimes, I have to instruct the interpreter how to say things or ask the questions. I ask for detailed explanation of the way that the questions translate, because some things do not translate well from English to Spanish. This can be a bit of an additional headache to the process. But it is an essential part of treating and evaluating Spanish-speaking work-injured patients. Make sure to ask the translators how each question is exactly worded, because if it is not worded correctly, the validity of the question posed is negatively affected.

When using translators, it is imperative to monitor how information is worded back to the patient. I regularly check at random to ensure that words are being translated properly. I have found there to be a wide range of skill level/personality in Spanish-language interpreters. Some of the most frustrating problems that I have encountered are when an interpreter arrives late or does not arrive at all, and the patient is stuck in the waiting room without an interpreter. Both you and the patient feel helpless and it is frustrating not being able to communicate. While this does not happen regularly, when it does happen it can be one of the most frustrating aspects of assessing and treating work-injured patients. Fortunately, I have not typically encountered any regular instances of Axis II problems with the interpreters. I did have one interpreter blow up at me when I politely asked him to stop using his phone during a session. The occasional examples of personality problems can be frustrating, but they do not occur with any regularity.

I do recommend that if you are seeing a patient for therapy who needs interpreter services that you attempt to keep the same interpreter throughout the course of their treatment. Many times the patient will want to keep the same interpreter because of their rapport with that person. Some of the things that they will be discussing will be difficult for them and they will want to have consistency. The consistency can diminish the iatrogenic anxiety that they experience when they first begin treatment. I have found that when a patient has the same interpreter present throughout treatment, they tend to do a better job with sharing and divulging important information. Ensuring that the patient is at least decently connected with their interpreter becomes a surprisingly important element in getting therapeutic results.

Now we need to discuss the financial side of reimbursements. Let's say that the reimbursement rate for your normal insurance patients for therapy is $120 per hour. Now let's say that by seeing work-injured patients, you are paid $150 per hour. This is a huge difference, while it initially doesn't look too exciting. Think about it this way . . . there is a big difference between making $120K and $150K annually. That's $30K difference. Not that you have to see all work-injured patients (and you may not want to, particularly if you don't have competence in this realm). But if you have ever seen work-injured patients in your training, please consider doing so in your private practice. You will be glad, both economically and professionally, that you did.

On Psych Assistants

You might want to consider having a psych assistant for your practice. Hypothetically speaking, having a good psych assistant is a way that you can increase the volume of work, which will be money in your door. While I have not chosen to hire a psych assistant, I sought guidance from multiple colleagues regarding this matter. I have received a variety of responses regarding what works best for having a psych assistant.

I chose not to be a psych assistant while I was in graduate school. The reason was consistent to the premise of this manuscript—in which my primary goal was to complete my program in as timely a fashion as possible. While I missed out on some income that I would have had doing psych assistant work, I decided that moving rapidly toward starting a private practice would be the best decision. Honestly, I felt that I was so busy during graduate school that I didn't have much time for extra work in psychology, other than my year-long predoc clinical placements. Once I was full-throttle into my dissertation, I certainly did not have many extra hours to do other work. And the extra hours that I had, I wanted to spend with friends, in attempting to practice adequate self-care. Some colleagues who have done psych assistant-ships have mentioned that they have gained a great deal of knowledge, expertise, and cash from their time spent as a psych assistant. They have also told me horror stories of individuals who have held psych assistantships and have worked hard, and have completed hundreds of hours, only to find out that their hours do not count toward licensure in their particular state. You definitely do not want to be in the position where you have worked hundreds of hours and do not have the correct percentage of supervised hours in which you have worked. Also, money is an important factor, as it is important to consider what kind of money you might make as a psych assistant, because there are big differences between being paid $15 and $30 per hour.

I have consulted with multiple colleagues who have taken on psych assistants. There are some rules that are important to follow, if you are considering adding a psych assistant for extra income. One colleague has mentioned that it is imperative to have quality control with psych assistants. For instance, the colleague saw them make many errors with analyzing test data. And then the colleague needed to take extra time to correct the errors and also to help the assistants, so that they do not make the same errors in the future. The colleague has mentioned that her cost in time (money) has not been worth having the psych assistants make errors on the test data. One colleague has mentioned that it is imperative to hire a good and competent psych assistant. She noted, "Oversight on what [psych assistants] do is important. I have seen scoring errors and major errors on the report. A psych assistant wants to learn so you need to remember to take responsibility for their work. If you want to use them, you have to be careful. Some of them do things, really noticeable mistakes, and it is your life on the line because you are signing off on them."

It is important to have many writing samples before you take a psych assistant on. For instance, if they are not strong in report writing, or if they don't have adequate training in writing reports, you don't want to take a lot of your time to help them improve. Be sure that the psych assistants are familiar with the testing instruments that you use. For instance, there have been some recent changes with new editions of the WAIS and WMS. If they are not familiar with the new instruments, you do not want to spend valuable hours teaching them the changes on the instruments. While it could be a meaningful or valuable experience helping them to learn the instruments, this book is about helping you maximize your earning potential. You also don't want to be in a situation where there is a lack of competence with a psych assistant, which could lead to a malpractice suit.

I don't think it is beneficial to take on a psych assistant so that you can play clinical supervisor. Remember that you have psych assistants to help your practice run more smoothly and efficiently, while creating extra income. You also want to be careful about whether the person plans on using their hours work to count towards postdoc hours. So some individuals may be working hours that are either supervised or unsupervised hours. Either way, the individual needs to be careful about what the requirements are for each state, as the number and percentage of hours supervised varies by state. Be clear regarding what the responsibilities and goals of the psych assistant are, and be sure that you can meet those requirements for them. For instance, in Washington State, you can't be a clinical supervisor unless you have three years post-licensure. So each state will vary in terms of their requirements for being a supervisor and whether you can have a psych assistant.

References

American Psychological Association. (2002). Child custody evaluations second most. Report of the Ethics Committee, 2001. *American Psychologist, 57,* 646–653.

Pickar, D. Child custody evaluations. Retrieved from http://www.danielpickarphd.com/publications/Child-Custody-Evaluator.pdf

Psychologists not accepting Medicare. (May 2010). Retrieved from http://www.apa.org/monitor/2010/05/medicare.aspx

8

MANAGING FINANCES

Spending

The checks are now coming in. I remember when I received my first check for more than $1K. It was exciting. Very exciting. I really felt like my hard work was finally paying off. I also recognized that I was going to be seeing many more checks for the same amount. Sure enough, I did. When I moved back to the Pacific Northwest from San Diego, I ended up purchasing a condo. The condo was not in a nice part of town and it was what I could afford at the time. It was in a very quiet building. The purchase ended up being an excellent decision. You don't want to have a huge amount of financial burdens on you when you are starting out. Let's do some simple math to illustrate my point.

When you begin your practice, you are going to have to set aside about $10K to pay for the psychological testing instruments. Take out a loan if you need to, but you will have to purchase these things. These are like tools for a mechanic . . . nothing short of a necessity. Let's say that you have a $200 payment on that. Maybe you have student loans. That might be a $500 payment. So we are already up to $700 a month based on necessities. And the sooner you begin paying for the student loans, the better. Do not put off paying them off, because you are just going to have to pay more in interest—kind of like handing the bank free money, which is never a good thing. You are also going to need a good, reliable car. There is never a good excuse for arriving late to your office, and it is just going to lose you business. When you are thinking of a car, don't only think about sexy. Think utility, think reliability, think reputation. Jaguar makes some nice-looking cars but they have made a very poor reputation for unreliability. I suggest that you check out Consumer Reports on their recommended models of cars. Consumer Reports typically rates the following cars as the most reliable: Honda Civic, Honda Accord, Toyota Camry, and Toyota Corolla. Reliability should be paramount. Please also ensure that you choose a car that you can pay for. If you choose a $35K car, you are going to have a $500 per month car payment. If you can't afford that, DO NOT PURCHASE A $35K–$40K CAR! Do not do that unless you have the income to work with the $500 monthly payment. Seriously, look into these things and, most importantly, choose a car that is reliable and one that you can afford. Wait until the money is really streaming in to purchase the cool car or take the posh vacation.

When you think about housing options, please consider rent/mortgage that is $1K or less. Seriously, this is not glamorous, BUT YOU ARE JUST STARTING OUT. Maybe you live with your partner or spouse and they are paying for it. Sweet deal. I wasn't as fortunate. But seriously, I know you want to live in the new construction condo with granite countertops and stainless appliances. So does everyone else. That's why more than half of Americans are buried in debt that they likely will never pay off. It is not easy finding a place where the rent/mortgage is going to be $1K per month. And if you are living in certain places, like LA, SF, NYC, that likely won't be possible . . . especially for a mortgage. But I strongly encourage you not to begin your practice in those densely populated areas. Look into it, and likely those areas are heavily saturated with successful psychologists. Consider living outside the city a bit, which will save you money and will likely leave you just as heavy a patient load. People need therapy/psych evals whether they live in the city or country.

There can be huge financial benefits from having a $1K mortgage as opposed to a $1.5K mortgage. Let's discover the tangible benefits. So if you have a $1K per year mortgage that is $12K per year. A $1.5K mortgage is $18K per year. So right there you are gaining $6K per year or $18K in three years. Guess what? You have paid for your psych tests right there. And you have paid to create a nicer office environment. In 10 years, that difference balloons to $60K . . . just a ton of money. Part about having a cheaper place to live when you are starting out is having the idea of deferred gratification. I mean, you won't have to live in your place forever. And when you are making more money, you can buy something else and potentially rent the place out which will provide you with some income. That's what I did, and now I have a renter in my condo and collect a check each month. Now I don't get huge rent check but it is money I have coming in each month. And that property is yours, so when this housing crisis gets better and property goes up again, it will be a nice tangible asset that you have. Honestly, for most portions of the United States, the current economic climate offers some tremendous buying opportunities—particularly with the amount of foreclosures and short-sales available on the market. Look into these things!

When you are looking for housing options, I strongly suggest finding an initial place that isn't next door to your office, but is in the close vicinity. I found a place that was about 10 minutes from the office. This meant that I had a very short commute and I could also get a bit more sleep each night. You don't want a place that is too close to work, because you want to be sure to separate your work and personal life. This is a very important part of self-help for psychologists. Staying somewhere right next to where you work is going to have you thinking of constant things to do at the office. And there are always things to do. Seriously, I could find a million things to do right now as I type on my computer.

If possible, I also strongly suggest that you consider a quiet location. My original condo was in an older building but it was very quiet as mostly elderly folks resided in the complex. Good call there. Look around and talk to the residents. Is there a lot of road noise outside? Is the place clean and somewhere you would like to come home to after a stressful day of work? Use your clinical intuition here. You want somewhere peaceful. The reason is simple. You will want some place that isn't chaotic, because starting a practice can be very stressful. You will want a place to come home where you can relax and meditate, if needed. And if you have children, you are going to be coming home to plenty of noise. If you are living somewhere where the person upstairs is noisy or keeps you up late with late-night festivities, that is going to likely weigh on you and will make it harder for you to work hard.

I would strongly consider that you buy your place. I know it is going to take 30 years to pay the thing off. And I know that my estimate of $1K per month for a mortgage is not going to apply to a condo in San Diego or NYC. But folks, you want to buy, rather than rent, if you can. When you buy you have a tangible asset on your hands. Buying is always a good call. It improves your credit and potentially you will be living rent-free. I will explain. So let's say that you purchase a condo for $130K. The payment on that might be around $1K per month. Let's say that the payment includes home-owner's fees. So you live in the condo for five to 10 years. Hopefully five or less years, since you will be doing so well in your clinical practice! When you are ready to sell your place, you sell your condo for $140K (assuming the housing crisis slightly improves at that time, as economic indicators currently suggest). Your condo has appreciated by more than 5 percent. Now you are going to have a ton of fees selling your place. But if you sell the place for $140K, you are going to pretty much break even when you factor in all of your fees to pay closing costs, real estate agent fees, etc. What have you done? You have just lived for five years in your condo FOR FREE! Yes, for free. Because you now have your money back that you invested in the first place. You can now reinvest that money in a better property. Plus, you have improved your credit by paying a monthly mortgage. Creditors like that kind of thing. It's likely that you will now be qualified to purchase a better place.

Where you live makes a major difference in how much you will pay for rent or a mortgage. Let's say that you are paying $1K for housing. So now you are up to $1,700 per month. That is not including over-head for the office, which I am assuming should be phone/internet $100 and rent $300. Now we are up to $2,100 per month. Add the $100 cell phone payment and you have $2,200 per month. That is a huge sum of money. You are going to have to make at least $2K to $3K per month to break even.

Look, this is looking pretty daunting on paper. But making $2K to $3K is going to be an easy task once you get started. Think about the state and government evals. If you do four evals for Social Security a month, you will make your money back. Let's say that you also do 10 state assistance evals at $130 a pop. Then you have now made $3,300. So you have $1,200 for your other living expenses. These expenses also include other costs of starting a practice, including paying for licenses, memberships, and miscellaneous costs. I am assuming that you are going to make more income on other psychological services that you provide but I just want you to understand how this will look by doing the bare bones amount of work to pay for things.

Do not accumulate credit card debt. Do not start a collection of Christian Louboutin shoes. This is simple economics. Do not use credit cards when you can't pay them off, unless you are both starving and homeless. Credit card debt is tough to pay off . . . especially when the rates get as much as 30 percent per month. So that $2K turns into 42.6K. That $3K in debt becomes $4K in debt. This is a huge difference. I would say that if you are really struggling and can't do anything about it, ask your parents for financial help. The worst thing that happens is that they say no. Do use your credit card regularly and make full payments on your credit card. This will improve your credit score and will help with you getting a loan on a house or condo. Do not make minimum payments on your credit card. If you don't have the money, don't spend it. And whatever you do, don't make lavish expenditures on your credit card thinking, "Oh, I will pay that off when I am making a lot of money." Sorry, that money is just going to keep going up and up and will be harder and harder to eventually pay off. I'm not saying don't use your credit card once you have become licensed. I'm saying, use it for essentials and for things that you can afford. Also consider having more than one line of credit. For instance, a credit card and a car payment equals two lines of credit. When you are applying for a home loan, banks are going to want multiple lines of credit, which will show them that you are responsible with making multiple monthly payments. It is a fine line, though, and if your income is too little and if your monthly payments are too much, it is going to be difficult to get that home loan. Basically, in 2013, we are stuck with banks not lending money, so obviously it is best to have the highest credit score possible, the most lines of credit and the least amount of debt. Basically, the banks want the moon. If you don't give it to them, they won't give you a home loan right now.

Saving

This is something that I feel very strongly about, so no BS here. You need to save money to protect your future. Let's say that you contract a disease that will force you out of working. Chances are this will never happen. But you will need money to live. And your parents probably won't be able to help you here. You really need to plan for all contingencies (sounding preachy here, but honestly, it is true).

Saving is so important. Let me explain why it can be a wonderful thing. Let's say that you start saving $100 a month at age 20. Now you probably didn't start doing this at 20 but my case only illustrates a point. If you invested $100 a month, based on a 10.25 percent return (pretty good return on investment here), you would be a millionaire by age 65. Pretty shocking stuff, huh? Another example is for parents. Parents, let's say that you start saving $100 a month for your kids when they are age 1. With an average return of 6 percent, your kids would be millionaires by age 65. Good deal, huh?

Another example of $100 a month. So let's say that you invest $100 a month and you get 8 percent return on your investment (which is still a very decent rate of return). Let's also say that you increase your investment by 3 percent each month, because you are going to be earning more and more money. By 10 years, your investment will be $21K, by 20 years your investment will be $65K and by 25 years your investment will be $101K. Pretty sweet deal here, as well, even with a lesser return. Seriously folks, you just may have to pay for your kids' tuitions. And those are not going to be cheap!

Do you think that you don't have $100 a month? I think so. This is easy stuff, people. Just buy a car that has a $100 cheaper payment. Or buy a condo that is $100 cheaper. So easy to save that kind of money. One other idea is to bring your lunch to work. Personally, I enjoy eating out, but look at the costs. If you spent $12 on lunch each day for a month that totals $240 per month. It is very likely that you will spend half of that by using groceries, so that will leave you with more than $100 a month in savings. See, saving is relatively easy. Another idea is to work harder. If you do one more psych eval a month that will give you another $500+ dollars. I definitely like the idea of working harder.

Try to set goals for this. And I mean attainable goals not aspirational goals. We aren't asking you to set aside $1K per month, people.

Try not to eat out as much or find very economical places to eat that are still healthy, like modest small cafes. If you can save $50 a week on eating out expenses, you can save up to $2.6K per year with that. That is a ton of money saved. Just think if you did that for five years . . . you would have $13K. Now that is a nice chunk of change to invest! Another idea is trying to cut down on needless expenses. Come on, do you really need that $30 haircut? Do you really need to buy *US Weekly* each week? Do you really need to buy two coffees per day? Take the latter. Let's say that you spend on the average $5 on coffee each day. That is $1.5K per year. Now what if you spend $3 per day. That is $900 per year. You just saved $600 a year, which equals $6K in 10 years. These are simple, common sense ways to save.

Another topic is taxes. You will have to pay a large portion of your earnings on taxes. Now there are plenty of tax benefits, like properly utilizing business expenses. But the bottom line is you are going to have to save for paying taxes, and it is going to cost you dearly. You will need to speak to your financial advisor on how much you should save for your taxes, depending on your income. Typically, this will mean one-third of your overall income. If you can save one-third of your income for taxes, you should be golden come tax season. There is nothing more important than paying your taxes as a business owner. You should know why people pay taxes. And there can be nothing worse than not being able to pay and having to pay penalty fees (incredibly steep, BTW). There are also benefits when you pay taxes where you can pay your taxes and also pay into your retirement. Plans such as a Simplified Employment Pension (SEP) work this way. You will need to talk to your financial advisor to learn more about this.

You will also have to pay a "Business and Operations" tax. While this varies from state to state, all small business owners, including clinical psychologists, have to pay this tax. I pay on a quarterly basis and it is nothing short than a pain in the ass. Talk about insult to injury . . . not only will you have to pay regular taxes, there will be additional taxes for being a small business owner. Please talk to your financial advisor about these things. You can't get out of them.

Professional Memberships

When you start your practice, please consider joining your state psychological associations. There are innumerable reasons for joining them, so I am going to highlight a few of them. It is good to have close colleagues and to be part of an organization. Join your state organization, because being in private practice can be quite isolating and you will meet some amazing people in the state association. I have been quite involved in my state organization, which has been an excellent decision for me. I enjoy socializing and "talking shop" with the other members. There are conferences that are interesting and meaningful. The people are so fantastic. You will meet people like Dr. Andy Benjamin, whom I met at a meeting of the Washington State Psychological Association. The man has a PhD and JD. He is nothing short of a brilliant guy. He is also incredibly generous with his time and gives a good deal of his time to helping other psychologists with ethical dilemmas . . . for free! Yeah, this is the kind of guy that you might meet in your state organization. So join because of the people.

Now for the other reasons. Networking. Networking. Networking. So much of business in our field is word of mouth. So network with your professional organization. I can't tell you how many calls I have gotten because I have been referred by another psychologist who doesn't see clients in my area. Network with these people. Talk to them, pick their brains, let them know about your training and experience. Don't be shy. I know this is going to be hard for some of you more reticent folks. But seriously, fake it if you can't do it well. Nobody will know that you are terrified to do this, I promise. If you really dislike any networking opportunities, please consult with your psychologist or psychiatrist, because this is an essential part of starting a practice. If you are afraid of talking with colleagues, consider talking to your psychiatrist about an anti-anxiety med. This stuff is important, because you are talking about free money and valuable enhancements to your practice. Neither is going to come to you unless you talk to others.

There are also tons of other advantages to being a member of your state organization. Benefits include continuing education opportunities (usually very cheap), legislative support (the organization usually has lobbyists that are out to protect the needs of psychologists at the state level and at the national level for APA), legal consultation (some state organizations offer free legal consultations), and ethics consultations (this is also free in some states). For all of these reasons, it is important that you join your state organization. While the dues usually aren't cheap, they are usually heavily discounted for those starting a practice. Being part of a state organization allows you to meet many different people from diverse backgrounds. These people may have some good input in terms of starting a practice. Ask around and get different opinions on getting started. Some will say that you should do everything yourself, while others will say that you should hire a secretary, or biller. Some will tell you about their early experiences as a psychologist, which are usually both helpful and interesting dialogues. One other benefit that I have found with the organization is that the members really care about the profession. They want you to succeed. With very few exceptions, at state conferences and meetings, there is a great energy around the place where people with passion and knowledge for our profession meet and greet. Soak up the information at the meetings and conventions.

The state association has social events where adult beverages are consumed (readily). These are good for networking and just venting about your workday. Ideas are bounced around with colleagues, simple consultation questions are answered, and other clinical topics are explored. Sometimes, we consult about cases. We all talk about things like our families or dating. These are all things that make us more human and less like psychologists. The content tends to be geared around psychology, but the time spent with friends and colleagues reminds you that it is OK to talk about other things. Talking about your friends' relationship problems feels good. Strongly consider utilizing this benefit of joining your state's psychological organization, as well. It feels good to get out and socialize! Now I have friends in psychology and outside of psychology. But there is just something rewarding about getting drinks with colleagues. I think it normalizes our lives. Definitely a healthy thing.

Benefits also include getting involved in the organization. For instance, I have served as a regional chapter president for the Washington State Psychological Association, which gave me other nice networking and consulting opportunities. Working with the psychological association has been really fulfilling. I was doing it in part because my job can be so isolating in private practice and I feel like more of a team when I work with the association. I have previously served as a co-chair of the Early Career Psychologists branch of the Washington State Psychological Association. In that position, I have attempted to help others with starting a practice, and responded to licensure questions and other issues faced by early career psychologists. I received emails from students wanting to know more about private practice, and I felt good that I can help them. I was blessed with some fantastic mentors who gave me some excellent guidance during my first years after I finished school. Please consider becoming involved in your state psychological association. I think you will be glad that you did. If nothing else, being involved is an opportunity to meet some really interesting and great people. Remember that having a private practice can be isolating, so being a part of a large organization is a good way to connect with colleagues. These organizations can break up the isolative work environment that you have on a daily basis.

Networking

Networking does not always come easy. Being a good schmoozer is not a natural skill for some people. As we know, people are born/socialized with different levels of introversion/extroversion. So if you are an extreme introvert, read on. For those who never struggle with socializing, I invite you to move on to the next section.

There is a custom in Japanese society from which we, as Westerners, can surely learn. In Japan, when you meet someone new, you give them your business card. And then you proceed to put their business card in your front right pocket. This shows that you respect the person that you just met and that you see the value in talking to them. It is a sign of respect, minus the kowtow. Western society can learn from that. When you meet someone, let them know that you value them. Show them respect, listen to what they say, and reflect what they said. This is not hard and should typically come naturally to us. I don't care if the person in question is a streetsweeper or a CEO. Talk to them and let them know that you value what they are saying. And if you don't value what they are saying, do your best to fake it. Network with people who are in similar occupations. For instance, it is more important for you to network with psychiatrists than with bankers. Psychiatrists, like psychologists, come in a wide range of shapes and colors. Some are fantastic people and others can be very difficult. Find the ones that you connect with well and continue the relationship. I have a few psychiatrists that I refer to and they also refer to me regularly. They have a good, grounded view of the patients' diagnostic considerations and are not simply giving everyone in their office a diagnosis of Bipolar Disorder Type I or Type II. These people are considerate and thoughtful and are good businesspeople. Make the extra effort to connect with your area psychiatrists, and you will be happy that you did when you receive a steady stream of referrals.

There are some (probably many) people in clinical psychology who are quiet and reticent. Research on the personalities of psychologists indicates that psychologists typically embody more introversion than extraversion. For some psychologists, being around others and socializing is exhausting. For others, there may be some predisposed social anxiety features that prevent them from socializing well. Still others may have other psychological issues that prevent them from communicating well or from connecting well with others.

When you are at social events, remember that you don't have to be perfect. Just do your best and that will be enough. Similar to your clinical practice, you aren't always going to say the right thing. Rely on your intuition here and use some of your clinical inference when you are talking to others. Ask them questions about things that you can infer are important to them. When you are talking to MDs, ask where they went to school, what that was like, how they like their practice. If you are talking to lawyers, ask them what kind of law they practice and what sparked their interest in the field. People typically enjoy talking about where they are originally from, so ask them that one, too. Just as you do with a therapy patient, consider implementing open-ended questions. This will allow the individual to elaborate on your queries.

I want to touch on two different aspects of communication. For some this will be an unnecessary review, and for others this may be helpful. When you are networking with others, be aware of 1) presentation and

2) content. Presentation means how you present when you are speaking in public and content refers to what you say. These are important things to be mindful of when you are meeting someone new.

There are some things to remember with your presentation. Dress nicely. Do not be slovenly dressed or poorly groomed at these networking opportunities. Wear something nice and professional. If you are a female, wear business appropriate attire. Guys should not choose the loudest shirt in their wardrobe. Wear simple, practical colors. I would also suggest wearing a suit or blazer. It is OK to wear a nice pair of good-looking jeans if you are a guy. But pair that with a blazer so that you look more dressed up. Women could wear dressy/designer jeans and a jacket, or the kind of professional attire they would wear to a business meeting, depending on their personal style. First impressions are important. I know that sounds trite, but it is true. Whether you are talking to the most- or least-educated individual out there, a first impression is important. Make good eye contact when you are talking to people. This helps them know that you are interested. Use mirroring skills so that if the individual is not making good eye contact, mirror them and use occasional eye contact. You don't want to be staring at someone who isn't looking back at you.

Smile and look engaged. If you are not interested in what they have to say, pretend to be enthralled. Don't look uninterested. Making sure that you are fresh and rested also ensures that you will make a good appearance, so don't go out partying the night before you are meeting someone important, like a good referral resource. Dress nicely. Consider wearing conservative clothes. We are talking about a first impression here. What you wear matters. We live in a shallow society where many people believe that dress tells a lot about you. While it may not be typically validated by clinical research, it reflects the world in which we live.

I was once told by my first clinical supervisor that you need to always dress nicer than the next person. I have strived to dress well throughout my time as a psychologist, and I have received good feedback for doing so. Appear confident when you are networking. Whether you are talking to a brain surgeon or his receptionist, act like you know what you are talking about. If you have some concerns regarding your confidence in social settings, consider employing some positive self-talk, such as,

"I am going to be OK," "I look good," or "I feel confident." You may also want to practice in front of a mirror or with a friend if you have some anxiety. If the person you are meeting disagrees with you, don't argue with them. Usually networking is pretty simple, but some people can be feisty.

In terms of content, plan ahead what you want to say. This is the same as preparing for a presentation. The more you prepare, the more confident you are going to be and likely the more appealing you will be to the listener. While it is OK to make some small talk, please don't say anything strange, don't make strange jokes—these things will only lessen your credibility and will make you less appealing to the potential colleague or referral source. You don't want to talk about the death of your mother or how your brother is addicted to sex. Keep your content positive. Try not to focus on negatives, unless you are trying to connect with other providers. For instance, I sometimes lament with other psychologists the difficulties with working with administrative issues for the state assistance program. This would be appropriate. Don't do anything dumb like call someone out for not having their top button buttoned.

Continuing Education

I previously explained how important it is to save your money. And just as important is to not spend your money on superfluous expenses. Attending continuing education (CE) events is not excessive spending. They can be great business write-offs. There are so many benefits of going to CE events. Let me explain. When you attend CE events, you are bolstering your knowledge. Particularly in psychological testing, there are always new tests coming out/new research on old tests. If you are doing any forensic testing, this will be particularly important to know the new research out there on the instruments that you are using, such as Rorschach, MMPI-2, Millon-2 and -3, etc. CE workshops provide excellent opportunities to bolster your knowledge base in the domains in which you are already versed.

But continuing education classes also provide a great chance to learn something new. Want to know a new technique to use when providing psychotherapy for teenagers? Wouldn't that be nice? Then go to the CE workshop for psychotherapy with teens. Acquiring new tools can be incredibly useful in your clinical practice.

There are some huge financial benefits from going to these events, because they can be written off 100 percent in terms of your travel costs or meals. Some entertainment will not be covered, such as attending a musical after the conference. But if you have dinner or lunch while attending the conference, that is going to count. And eat out somewhere nice! These are huge tax benefits and could really save you a ton of money on your vacations (CE trips). Most of the time, you are allowed to bring your spouse as well. If you want to know more about the tax benefits of attending CE workshops, please call your financial advisor or tax person. They will be able to fill you in with details about what is allowed and what isn't.

Finally, I would have to say that another intrinsic benefit of attending the workshops is the opportunity to meet some fascinating people. Sure, some people in our profession suck. Isn't that true of every profession? But honestly, I have found that by attending conferences and workshops I have met some really fantastic and interesting human beings. Take, for instance, Joseph. Joseph lives about an hour from my practice and we both have very similar practices. We were at breakfast at one of the Washington State Psychological Association conferences and I started talking to the guy. We start chatting about our personal lives and then talk about our clinical practices. Turns out, that the guy has pretty much the identical clinical practice as mine.

Joseph has a lot of really interesting things to offer about psych testing. First of all, he has been in his practice for 10 years longer than I have, so he is more seasoned and experienced. The guy is hilarious and we joke around about the lighter side of our work . . . which can be taxing, sometimes especially when you are talking about terminating parental rights. Not exactly a Disney film. While I don't get to meet with Joseph as much as I'd like, he is a referral source for me and we have referred to each other. Sometimes, we consult if there is an interesting clinical question. Bottom line is that a big bonus of attending CE workshops is the chance to meet really great people. Who knows, you might meet someone who has a practice just like you and thinks just like you. You might meet a lifelong friend. I highly recommend doing more CE units than what your state requires . . . don't just do the required amount. Remember, you don't want your license to lapse because of not completing your CE requirements. There is so much to learn and gain by going to the events. And the best part is Uncle Sam will pay for a substantial portion of what could be a fantastic vacation!

Pro-Bono Work

Everyone should do some pro-bono work. This book is about building a financially successful practice, so obviously you can't do all your work for free. But strongly consider seeing at least a few therapy patients for free each week or every two weeks. I do and it is incredibly rewarding. It is a well-known fact that people who are underprivileged do not receive adequate mental health care. I urge you to help improve this problem. Think about it for a moment, do you really not have time to see one or two more patients every two weeks or every month on a pro-bono basis? That can't be a no.

My state psychological association has a pro-bono pledge. This is a great thing and I understand that other states implement the same pledge. Seeing people for free is not something that you have to do. But it feels good to give back when you are financially ready to do so. When you have been practicing for a year or more, think about seeing a few people for free. And if you are really altruistic, do it right after you get licensed. I think that if every psychologist saw one pro-bono patient a week, we would be really making a difference in improving our community's mental health. This is a similar concept to recycling. One person does make a difference and an even greater difference can be felt when people catch on to improving society.

Work Ethic

I might be sounding a little preachy here, but I can't believe the major discrepancies in work ethics that exist with psychologists. I have a colleague, Dr. Tim Popanz, former Washington State Psychological Association president. Tim is a great guy. He works amazingly hard and has built his reputation on having an incredible work ethic. The guy sees eight (or sometimes more) patients for therapy each day, which is very impressive. Being perceived as a hard worker is never a bad thing.

As I write this, I have just completed a day-long evaluation. And it is a Sunday morning. I have gone the extra mile for this one, working all day and night Friday, part of Saturday, and part of Sunday. But that's what you have to do sometimes. I am going to argue that going the extra mile and working harder than your peers is essential in creating a financially successful private practice in psychology. I have been told my referral sources that I work harder than my peers. Do you think that the police department is going to like that I worked over the weekend? That I went the extra mile to complete the evaluation? People see these things. It is a good way to get repeat business. This is what pays the bills. It is what pays for trips to NYC or So Cal. It is what will pay for your daughter's wedding (well, not all at once, but after time!).

There are people who work four days a week, see five patients a day, and then never work on the weekends. They are making $60K. I don't do that. I have the financial rewards to prove it. Now they may have a slightly lower stress level than mine. But these are the extra things that you are going to need to do. They are going to be forced to have their kids pay for their own college. They are going to take forever to pay off their mortgage. They are going to drive the broken-down car, have their house in a bad neighborhood, and never eat out for dinner. If you want that lifestyle, do not work hard. If you don't want that kind of lifestyle, work very hard. Do you want to be the one making $60K a year? Maybe you don't care. But not likely. Work hard or try to work harder than your colleagues and that won't happen.

Now I know what you are thinking . . . "Get a clue, you have just started your practice. Wait until you are older and then you won't be working as much." But it is not about your career 20 or 30 years down the road. It is about building your practice, earning a good reputation as a hard worker and competent referral source, preparing for your family planning, and your children's tuitions. This is building a cornerstone for your future. Affording that trip to Maui. You will need to work very hard in your first few years to achieve that.

Now others might proclaim, "What are you talking about? I worked my ass off for licensure and now I am just going to work 20 hours a week. I am a psychologist after all." To me that sounds lazy. What I am hearing is that you exhibited a great work ethic throughout your graduate training and licensure and now you are going to throw that away and not work hard? What about your student loans? You think they can wait? What about your car payment, your condo mortgage? Is daddy going to pay for that? Is your husband or wife going to bail you out? Possibly. But not likely. Look, do not let your good work ethic slip. You have gotten this far. You have already accomplished a lot. Just keep it going. Honestly, once you get going, the money is there for the taking. You will have to work hard for your money and for your career satisfaction, but it will be well worth it.

I would argue that working hard is of intrinsic benefit to the soul. You can feel good about working your ass off for a psych eval. And then you can reward yourself when you are done and enjoy your free time. We are talking about having a better quality of life . . . for you and your family. Now I am not saying that you should be OCPD. If you are bordering on that spectrum of behavior, take a look in the mirror. Working very hard does not mean that you have to be OCPD. It just means that you have to go the extra mile sometimes. In my example a few paragraphs back, the police department had told me that they wanted the evaluation done by the weekend. I saw the patient all day Friday, worked on the eval some on Saturday, and some on Sunday. Now is this really an impossible task to do once every month? Prioritize it. If you have kids, take a little time away from the family to do it. Having some flexibility here can be key. It can make the difference in receiving regular referrals. Because the police department was pleased about my work ethic, I can look forward to a great relationship with them and many future referrals. Again, recognize the difference between having a good work ethic and having OCPD. I have a friend who just works all of the time to stay away from other things. Remember balance in your life. If you are bordering on OCPD (and you totally know who you are!) be mindful of that. Make changes and seek therapeutic interventions. Make sure that you have adequate ways to manage stress and if you are overworking to avoid contact with your wife, mother, or another family member, be mindful of that. Working hard is a way of life. And people are going to take notice and will respect you. But more importantly, you will respect yourself.

Referrals

My clinical practice is now full. This is fantastic. So I send people to other psychologists in the area. They appreciate this. I don't get sent roses or anything like that, but when I see colleagues, they thank me. If you are sent a referral, please thank them. They just basically handed you over a check. Thank them for that check. Put in a call or send them an email thanking them. The same is true for all referrals that you get, whether they are from a social worker or MD. People today are not as good at following through with social graces. A little old-fashioned gratitude will go a long way for you. There is also the chance that if you do not thank the person for their referral, you will not be seeing any more referrals from them. That would be a shame. Seriously, it is worth the minute or two of thanking them.

Also call the people who are referring to you. Talk to them about the cases and consult with them. Make sure to make your presence in the case known. Whether you are talking to a MD or nurse, stay in touch with the people referring to you. But don't only call; go and visit them sometimes at their offices. Now, I know that you can't do that regularly because of time issues, but seriously consider meeting with a referral source face to face. This is the old-fashioned way of doing business. And you know, especially if your referral source is an older man or woman, they will like that you made the time to go see them. We live in a cyber-world where email and fax is how we communicate. The profession of clinical psychology is built on spending face-to-face time with people. We need to continue to carry out this tradition with the people who we work with, not only with the people we see in our offices. The referral source will also see you as someone who goes the extra mile to get to know them and they will likely categorize you as someone who is "good" rather than someone who is "adequate," simply based on the effort that you give. They also may want to know how the patient is doing in therapy, so it is important to include a treatment plan with them and to keep them up to date with how the patient is functioning psychologically. Sometimes, they will also want a phone call about how the person is functioning emotionally. Make sure that you get a release from the patient so that you can speak to their referral source. The patient will likely appreciate that you are collaborating with the referral source. Think about the specialists in the community that can give good care for the patients. Remember that there are going to be clinical areas in which you can't or don't want to work. You have to be careful with not seeing clients that are outside your scope of abilities.

Working with the referral sources also means that you will not only be working with the medical doctors, psychologists, or other professionals, but you will be also working with their staff. Like people from a variety of professions, there are going to be good receptionists and then you will find those with Axis II traits/disorders (full-blown, in rare cases). Honestly, in the past few years, I have never really had any issues with office staff. I don't care if they talk to you like they just went through a tumultuous divorce, be nice to them, NO MATTER WHAT! They might want to talk to you about psychology, just as your cousin or friend does. Just say a few things with them and be cordial. Make small talk with them and if you really don't like them, then fake it! Remember, office staff are offering you referrals and they work for the people who are referring to you. If you don't get along with them or if you have an issue with them, the people who are referring to you won't like it. Nearly all of the time the staff are nice, genuine people.

Sometimes, the staff may be impatient if you don't get back to them immediately. So get back to them as soon as you can when you get a referral. Try to make timeliness in this domain a priority. Don't only thank the referral source for the referral, but thank the staff as well. The absolutely last thing that you want here is to have a negative interaction with a staff member and then they tell the medical doctor and then you don't get referrals from them anymore. What a disaster. You will be walking away from free money if you do that. So don't do that. Just be nice to everyone and you will be fine.

Sometimes, I will drop by the office of those who regularly refer to me. I have a medical doctor friend/colleague whom I have known for many years and I sometimes stop by to "check in" with him. Since he also works in interpersonal isolation in his private practice, he truly enjoys visiting and catching up. We talk about our families and we also talk shop. Consult with these people and remember your "presentation" and "content" when you are with them. Don't be afraid to throw out some psychological terminology. At the same time, don't use ridiculous psychobabble such as "hysteria" or "lability." Spending time with the referral source is time well spent. Please consider doing the same once you have built relationships with others who refer to you. We are talking about both opportunities for clinical growth and also money in your pocket. Both are essential for starting a successful practice.

Reputation

Sometimes, people are too focused on what others think about them. I have been guilty of this more than once in my lifetime. OK, maybe twice. But seriously, it is important to build a good reputation once you have started your clinical practice. I have built a reputation in my area as someone who is competent and who works hard. Of course, sometimes I get negative feedback. You are not always going to get positive feedback, especially if you opt for working with lower-functioning clients. But your reputation may earn you a good amount of referrals. I have been fortunate to earn a good reputation with a few medical doctors in the area, and they refer to me regularly. They have received good feedback from people that I have seen for psych evals or therapy, and so I am instantly associated with someone the referral source can trust. This doesn't mean that you have to suck up to everyone you see. I am just saying that if you are not working as hard as you can in your clinical practice, it is likely that others are noticing that. This is certainly something that is not essential in building a $100K+ practice, but it makes it considerably lot easier to be a solid earner when you are getting referrals left and right.

There is a difference between showing confidence and being a jerk. And you know the people in our profession who are confident and those who are overconfident. Don't be the person who thinks that he/she knows everything. That is just going equate to a poor reputation.

It is OK to appear confident at networking events and conventions. But don't pretend that you know everything. Be cognizant of how much you are talking about yourself. Just be aware of these things. Don't be afraid to mention some skills you have acquired but there is a fine line.

Finding a Teaching Job

Teaching doesn't pay. I thought that once I was licensed, I would look for teaching positions. I found one and was hired. While the work can be very meaningful, guess what, folks, the teaching jobs don't pay. Let's revert to some simple math. OK, let's say that you get paid $5K for the semester. Let's say that you are teaching for 15 weeks. Well, you have to teach a three-hour class for 15 weeks. That is 45 hours. Let's just say that you were getting paid hourly by just showing up there and teaching. That's $5,000/45 = $111 per hour. Now that is adequate pay for a psychologist. Again, teaching is not a good means to foster a financially successful private practice in psychology. I am not saying that teaching isn't incredibly valuable and meaningful work. I am saying that it doesn't pay the bills as well as your clinical practice will.

You may think that you are going to be paid for just the three hours that you are in class. But you are going to be working far more than that in your teaching job. Now we are going to be realistic. I estimate that you will be spending at least two hours a week on preparation for the class. If you are teaching a new class, there will be a ton more work than the two hours, but let's do the math again. Add 30 hours to that 45 and you have a total of 75 hours of work. That's $5,000/75 = $67 per hour. Now this is starting to really suck. That's Master's-level money. You didn't write that dissertation for $67 an hour. Did you? But just in case you are new teaching a class, it is going to take a lot more than two hours a week for prep. It took me probably at least six hours a week for prep. Now granted, I had never taught the course before, but let's do the math again. If you are constructing new lectures, this is reality, folks. It is going to take at least six hours a week outside of your teaching to write up a good lecture. So we already have the 45 hours where you will be teaching.

Now add 90 to that. You now have 135 hours. So we will do the math again, $5,000/135 = (get ready to cry) . . . . $37 per hour. This is not good stuff. Now, these figures are even more disconcerting for those living in areas where the cost of living is expensive, like San Francisco, LA, NYC, DC, etc. Really, folks, those mortgages and car loans and student loans are going to have to be paid for. You can't wave your magic wand and say, "Voila, disappear!"

Now let's do a simple comparison here. Why don't we say that out of those 135 hours you were getting half clinical hours (67.5). And let's say that you are getting $120 an hour for each clinical hour. That's 120 X 67.5 = $8,100. So let's get this straight, if you were only doing half the amount of work (67.5 clinical hours, as opposed to 135 hours working on teaching the class), you would be making more than $3K more in the same time period. I was never a math major, but this just makes A TON OF SENSE! If you want to make money, really think about these things. Now try this: let's say that out of the 130 hours that you would work for a semester of teaching, you spent two-thirds of that time doing clinical work. We are talking about 85.8 clinical hours here, rather than the 67.5 clinical hours or one-half the amount of hours that you would be spent teaching. So we will do the simple, basic math again . . . $120 per hour x 85.8 = $10,296. Now we are talking! So if you spend two-thirds the amount of time that you would have spent teaching doing clinical work, you will make MORE THAN DOUBLE WHAT YOU MAKE TEACHING. I think I've proved a point. I am not saying that you have to work like a madperson. I am simply making the argument that teaching does not pay when you are starting out as a clinical psychologist.

Teaching doesn't pay unless you get a very large research grant. Which could happen. In that case, teaching may be very profitable. There is also a possibility that teaching will get you more patients because of your reputation as a professor. The more you are known, the more people will be coming in your door. I'm not sure that having a teaching job will help build your practice. I think that you can also argue that having a teaching job will take away time where you could be marketing or networking. It might take away time from your private practice, which is the best way to make money in psychology when you are starting out. I'm not writing this section to say that you shouldn't teach. In fact, I am currently an affiliate professor at Trinity Lutheran College, a four-year college in the Seattle area. But I am just saying that it is highly unlikely that teaching will be a good way to create a financially successful private practice after you are licensed.

9

SELF-CARE

Taking Care of Yourself

Our work is stressful. Seriously, strongly consider going into therapy. It can be a great way to both vent and consult. Sometimes, it is always a good idea to bounce an idea off of another psychologist. Consider getting occasional massages. And if you are not a massage person, treat yourself to a nail or hair salon, or whatever makes you happy. Under certain financial limitations, of course. Getting a massage doesn't mean getting a massage every week. If you get one massage a month at $100 a pop, that will be $1,200 per year (unless insurance helps), and that is not an insignificant expense. So, if you can't pay that, get one every two months.

Taking care of yourself also includes planning occasional weekend escapes. Take time to go on that hiking trip with your significant other. My weekend time is spent recharging. Whether I am out with friends or sitting watching professional soccer highlights, I enjoy my weekend time and I try to make the most of it. If you enjoy having a pedicure, get a pedicure. Do what is comfortable to you. Make sure to regularly do things that you enjoy. Don't do lavish things, but just do things that will help you cope with a stressful job. I highly recommend spending time with quality people, like friends and family.

Finding balance also means working on things outside of psychology. Consider doing some pleasure reading or taking a class on something that interests you. We get so engrossed in our daily work that sometimes it can be hard to work on other areas of interest. I have a friend and colleague who enjoys taking guitar lessons. And he's gotten much better in the past few years. Consider doing something like that. It can be challenging or it can be just fun. If you are up for a challenge, test yourself. If you want to do a relaxing activity, that is fine, too. Some people love spending time with pets as a way to unwind or relax. If you are a pet person, make sure to schedule time with them. Join a Zumba class or volunteer at the local food bank. This can also be a great way to meet people from outside of psychology. Some people find pleasure in cooking or hosting dinner parties. I enjoy having people over for dinner or BBQs, and that can be a way for me to unwind and also catch up with friends. I have found these times with friends to be invaluable for me.

It is important to set good boundaries for yourself. Some of you might have the tendency to get involved in too many things. Volunteering yourself for activities that you can't complete will make you feel overwhelmed. I have always worked at finding a good balance with my activities. I have enjoyed being a part of the Washington State Psychological Association, but I have been careful not to overextend myself with responsibilities in the association, since I have a full clinical practice and also currently teach undergrad psychology part-time. Some of you may struggle with saying no to things. Please work on this issue. Just as you might struggle with saying no to the person up-selling you at the Verizon Wireless store, you might also struggle with involving yourself in too many tasks or positions. Start paying attention to your body and how it reacts when you are stressed out with too many activities. If you feel too stressed out, limit your activities and step down from one of your commitments. While the group or organization might be initially disappointed by you doing that, simply tell them that you have to be better at knowing your limitations. Communicate with them that you have felt stressed out and they will likely understand. This actually happened at one of my Washington State Psychological Association meetings. It was a friend of mine who held a leadership position there and he was starting to feel overwhelmed with the amount of work that he had in his practice, his position at the psych association, and also other stuff in his personal life. He was overworked and could not perform well at the association. It took a good deal of bravery but he told the entire leadership council why he needed to resign from his position. But he showed heart and courage, and the group reacted very well to his resignation. He had worked hard for the association but was overstressed and couldn't continue. People understood and we filled the position with someone else. So know your limits, and if you are feeling too overwhelmed or stressed out with your activities, you need to work on limiting what you are doing. Otherwise you might bear the physical and mental consequences of your over-involvement.

We talk about the importance of diet and exercise with our patients. Eat well and exercise regularly. These are great ways of taking care of yourself. A healthy body is a healthy mind. I know it sounds trite, but that's what the research indicates. If you are out of shape, consider getting in shape ASAP. People are coming to you for advice and they will likely judge you if you are obese. We live in a shallow society where people who are overweight are automatically deemed as unacceptable or lazy. Don't allow yourself to fall in this category. Sadly, if you are obese, you could be missing out on some serious referrals, because society likes people who are an appropriate weight. But do this for yourself. I am just being brutally honest here. How can we recommend adhering to a diet and exercise program for an obese patient when we are overweight ourselves? That just makes us look bad. Be careful about what you eat, what you take in, and what you burn off. If you exercise five days a week for 30 minutes a day and adhere to a relatively careful and healthy diet, you should not be overweight . . . with a few exceptions. And take advantage of the benefits of exercise. We have stressful jobs and exercise can be a huge stress relief. Recent studies have indicated that exercise can be as effective as taking anti-depressant medication. Sometimes our work is downright depressing. There is really no good reason to not exercise regularly, unless you suffer from some grave physical ailments.

Practice good hygiene. Make sure to have enough sleep each night. On the nights before you are not working, having good sleep is not quite as important but make sure to get 6–8 hours of sleep, minimum, when you are working the next day. You want to be sharp each day at work and getting enough sleep is going to help you reach your financial goals. You will not be as sharp, cognitively, without a good night of sleep. Continual nights of poor sleep also make your cognition suffer even more. Do not sell yourself short here. For those who have major sleep issues/sleep disorders, please get help for the issues. Maybe it will require psychiatric medications. If nothing else, go in for a consultation with your primary care physician. If you don't think that you need medicine, work on mindfulness/relaxation training. There are a multitude of good books on this, including *Full Catastrophe Living* by Jon Kabat-Zinn. This book will help you with tension and will help relax your mind and body so you get to sleep. You may also want to get a book on sleep disorders to help you learn more about the problems.

Try to spend time in the sun. Being in your office with artificial lighting can be downright damaging to your health. Everyone needs a little Vitamin D, so try to spend some time in the sun every few days (if possible and not living in Nome, Alaska). If you don't live in a sunny place, spend some time where it is sunny. For instance, I live in the Seattle area and I try to spend time in Southern California a few times per year to recharge my batteries. I can tell when I need sunshine and going down there helps me refocus my energy so that when I come back to a full clinical practice I feel invigorated. Sunlight also increases the production of positive endorphins in the brain so the biochemical aspect of being in sunlight is important to note as well.

Keep yourself well hydrated when you are working during the day. Many studies point toward how keeping yourself hydrated helps immunity and energy, and prevents illness. It just makes sense that cells need water for them to function properly. Protect yourself during the cold and flu seasons by getting a flu shot, drinking plenty of water, and taking vitamins. During the fall and winter months, I always pump myself full of vitamins, particularly B vitamins and vitamin C, which help with immunity and also provide energy. I would consider doing this even if you reside in a sun-belt region, like Florida or Southern California, as the flu travels everywhere. There are many studies out there that indicate that those vitamins can help with ageing, mood, and energy. I think it is not surprising that many of my patients report that they feel better when they take B and C vitamins. I would also recommend adding more vitamins during particularly stressful times during your life—such as during a separation from a relationship, a death in the family, or other life-related traumas.

Manage stress the best way that you know how. If you are working exceptionally long hours, make sure to take time after you see patients to be good for yourself. Do this EVERY DAY! Some people love taking baths, some love hitting the gym (me), others like shopping (could be trouble). Maybe try yoga or meditation. Research indicates that these can be very helpful ways to cope with stress. But seriously, self-care is so important in our profession. My psychologist would also query me about my self-care and sleep hygiene. She was right to get on me, because I work a good amount each week and it is important for me to take care of myself. And I have been good to myself because I recognize that my own sanity could be compromised if I don't have good self-care. I find lifting weights a great stress relief. If you have never done any weight-lifting, I suggest you try it. You might find it empowering and a great way to blow off steam after a day at the office.

Monitor yourself if you are finding less appropriate ways to manage stress: that extra glass of wine or that cigarette. These are not healthy ways to cope with a stressful profession. Talk things over with your friends and colleagues. Make sure to connect with colleagues regularly. I have a psychologist friend who has told me that his best therapist is his wife. Now I definitely think that it is a good idea to be able to talk to your significant other, but I wouldn't recommend dumping all of your stuff onto him/her. Talk about projective identification! Bounce ideas around people who are in the field. And it is OK to joke around with them about someone you saw professionally. There can definitely be hilarity in our field.

I feel that there is no harm in watching mindless TV. Sometimes I just get home and I want to watch junk on TV. I am typically a sucker for sports highlights. I don't see a huge problem with this, as long as I am not doing that all of the time. Reading can also be a great way to unwind . . . as long as the reading materials are light and relaxing. I wouldn't recommend reading horror books after a hard day at work, unless you have a masochistic bent. For me, as an extrovert, time with friends is a great stress reliever. My job can be very isolating, so I look forward to the weekend time with friends. Plan fun things to do with friends to cope with the monotony of the workweek, which sometimes can be overwhelming. When you have Thursday happy hour planned on Monday, it can make the workweek go more quickly. If you have a significant other, plan fun dates for convenient times. This is another thing to look forward to. If you have kids, plan time with your significant other away from kids. Get a babysitter occasionally and go out and have fun.

Some people like to play on their phones and can spend hours playing games on their phone or computer. I think that if you are stressed out, there can be some cathartic value with doing that. And also with texting. Texting is kind of a half-relationship or half-conversation with someone. If you need to get something out about your stressful day, you'll probably get better value out of a face-to-face conversation or a talk over the phone than texting. But I think that some people prefer to vent over text, which can be helpful for some people. Just remember that people are not going to always understand the meanings behind your texts and if there is meaningful content it might be best discussed over the phone or face to face.

Consider starting therapy with a skilled psychologist. This will be a good way to vent about your (probably) hectic life. While I am not currently in therapy, I have been in the past and it has helped me through personal issues and professional issues. I looked forward to therapy like I would to a massage or to a great meal. Make sure to find a psychologist who is a good fit for you. If you are seeing someone who is not a good fit, stop immediately and see someone else who is. This is an easy choice, because you don't want to throw out your money somewhere that you don't feel comfortable. Use your clinical inference here and if you don't feel good about therapy, go see someone else. Of course we know that not every therapist is a good fit for each particular person. The same should be true with you.

Know what your body is telling you, if you are stressed out. If you are getting sick, remember to take breaks during the day, and, if necessary, take the day off and get better. This is a hard one for me, because I tend to not want to take days off. When you take days off, you don't get paid, as you only get paid for people that you see in a private practice. Even though I don't like the idea of financial loss, I am careful to listen to my body if I am feeling badly, because things will likely get worse if I don't and I will be out even more money. I also don't like the idea of telling patients that I can't see them for their scheduled appointment—especially those who really need help. But sometimes I have to think about my capabilities and if I am not able to provide patients with a high level of care because of sickness, I try to reschedule them. So listen to your body and then decide whether you need to take the day off because of illness.

Taking Breaks During the Day

So this is also connected to the previous topic, taking good care of yourself. I have a colleague who will see seven patients a day for 45-minute sessions and won't take any breaks for herself. She has a family and really values her family time, but it is pretty hard to believe that she does not take regular breaks. The woman works really hard but it is not something that I would recommend. While she doesn't work every day, she may be prone to future burnout for her lack of taking breaks.

Taking breaks between therapy patients is a way to refresh and recharge. I regularly surf the internet between patients. Those 10–15 minutes are quality time that I get to spend by myself. And sometimes I return phone calls or do some work-related chores on my breaks, but a lot of the time I am working on recharging for the next person. I do the same thing between psych evals. I take regular breaks and that helps me refocus.

Really consider taking a lunch break every day. I take an hour lunch break and it is a perfect way to break up my day. Lunch breaks are essential, because your brain will be needing food to function as well as it can. If you don't eat lunch, you won't be as sharp as you can be. I take a bit of a longer break than many people do, but I look forward to it every day. If you don't want to take an hour break, take a 30- or 40-minute break. This is just part of being good to yourself. Taking breaks will also help you get recharged to continue your day. Research on attention and concentration indicates that we are really only at our best for an hour or two each day at a time (depressing, huh?). So if we work eight hours straight, we are definitely not going to be at our cognitive best. Recognize your limitations here. While a person's ability to concentrate for a given period of time is pretty variable, you can't really concentrate well for eight straight hours, can you? If you said yes, you are probably lying. Make sure to take breaks during the day.

When a patient no-shows (and unfortunately, there will be plenty of these in your practice), consider taking a break. Sometimes I find it hard to take a break when there are ton of things for me to do, such as answering phone calls, revising evaluations, or doing bookkeeping work. Consider taking a short nap when you have a patient no-show. I have found this to be particularly invigorating and energizing for the rest of the day—particularly when my no-show is at 2 or 3 PM and I am working until 6 PM. Usually, what I do is I put in ear plugs so that I block off noise, lean back in my chair with my legs resting on the couch, and I start a visualization of being in a relaxing spot for vacation. I get in touch with my senses, which calms me and sometimes puts me to sleep. Consider doing this occasionally, rather than returning that phone call.

You might consider taking more time off once your practice is thriving. There might be life circumstances that would require you to take more significant amounts of time off. Circumstances include the death of a spouse, marriage, or childbirth. These are life circumstances that we can't always prepare for. And they seriously interfere with maintaining a financially successful private practice. Let's say that you have to shut down your practice for one year because of a childbirth. The birth of a child is priceless and it is something that you will never forget. Being with that child during the first few years of his or her life is a blessing, and one of the best things in life (for many). But remember that if you stop your practice for more than one year, you will likely have to start from the beginning once again. Even if you do a part-time practice, it is going to take a great effort to build your practice up to full time again.

Raising Children

You want to consider these things before you start your practice. Now, as a disclaimer, this book is about being financially successful and these are things that you might want to consider. If you are a female and want children (and want them soon), you have to be aware that having children will negatively interfere with becoming financially successful in your private practice. Raising children will also be something that you will likely have to budget for, as most middle-income families spend $12K per year on an infant. Just paying for baby food, formula, and diapers will cost you roughly $50 per week ($2.4K per year) alone. So these are things to really budget for, if you plan on starting a family while you have a thriving private practice. I am definitely not saying that you should not have a family. What I am suggesting is that you prepare for these life events by saving and communicating with your spouse.

You might want to consider the timing of having children, and while sometimes you cannot predict the timing, having children years after you have set up a financially successful private practice might be the best course of action. This is a very complicated matter, as I have had multiple female psychologist colleagues who have taken different stances on this. For instance, I have one colleague who is adamant that you should have children before you start your private practice. And certainly many female psychologists have gone this route and have been financially successful. I have a colleague who mentioned that she was tired of waiting to have kids and started a family during graduate school. On the other hand, I have some other female psychologist colleagues who contend that it is best to wait to have children, until you have completed graduate school and have become licensed, or have already built a successful private practice. Following the careers of those colleagues who have waited to have children, I tend to agree with their model as the best way to become financially successful and reach a maximum earning potential, while having children.

I think that the answer for some may be somewhat dependent on the age of the practitioner, and might also depend on the income of the spouse. Let's say that your spouse makes $80K per year and you want to take three years off to raise your children. You would want to be sure that the $80K would be enough to support you and your child/children during that time. $80K after taxes is roughly $65K. Minus $12K for a baby leaves the family $53K for all other expenses. This isn't a ton of money for two people, but it might be doable, depending on where you live. If rent/mortgage is $1.5K per month, that leaves you with $35K for all other expenses. Now we are getting into difficult territory. $35K for a family's expenses is not a great amount. Things are even more difficult if you have three children. Three children with a spouse's $80K income, including a 1.5K per month rent/mortgage, leaves the family with only $11K per year worth of other expenses. That seems less doable and it might mean that you will need to work at least part-time. In the same scenario, with your spouse making $120K and having three children, you will be left with $96K after taxes, minus $36K for the three children is $60K, and minus the $1.5K per month rent/mortgage is $42K. That seems a lot better for taking care of all other expenses.

A highly successful female colleague of mine tells me that it is imperative to consider the financial costs of kids before you have kids. She has mentioned that you don't want to be in a situation where you are working 50 hours a week and not sleeping enough, while raising children. She notes that having children is mentally challenging and that working 40–50 hours per week, while raising children, might be too mentally taxing for most women. She cited another colleague in this situation that negatively affected her self-care. Self-care and work-life balance is essential when you are raising children. The same colleague is adamant about being or attempting to be financially stable before you have children, and I agree with her stance.

You can't always predict having triplets. But you want to budget for all of these things if you are considering having a family while you set up your financially successful private practice. Be prepared that if you take three to five years off to raise your children, it will take at least one year to restart a financially successful private practice. I think it will take roughly one year, even if you have a part-time, 10-hour-per-week private practice while you are raising your children. Even the most motivated and entrepreneurial psychologists need at least one year to set up a financially successful private practice. But let's set up the part-time scenario, just so that we can explore that option. You might be thinking that having a 10-hour-per-week private practice might be a good compromise between closing down your practice while raising children and keeping a full practice while raising children. Assume that your full practice includes working 40 hours per week, and that you make $100K per year out of that 40 hour per week private practice. That means that in a 10-hour-per-week part-time practice, you will make $25K per year. That might be a good option if your family is financially strained, or if you have the time to do it. If you have three children, this might not be an option, because you might be too busy. It is also going to be important for you to ensure that there will be someone to watch the children while you are working part-time. If your spouse has a 9–5 job, it might make sense to find a sitter or have a family member watch the children a few times per week.

I have a psychologist colleague who works part-time and has three children. Her husband works full time and is a medical doctor, so she is not able to work full time because she wants to spend the maximum amount of time with her children, while maintaining a part-time practice. Her situation is unique, because she is financially secure with her husband's $150K+ income. She has relationships with people in the community who refer to her and she wants to maintain those relationships by working part-time. My colleague works two days a week and roughly eight hours each day that she works, which lowers her overhead. Basically, she works very hard on the days that she works. She rents an office space for each day that she works, so she isn't stuck paying for a week's worth of overhead. This cuts down her expenses and is highly recommended if you are considering working part-time while you raise your children. She has family watch her children on the days that she works, which also greatly cuts down her expenses. Finding a good and reliable babysitter is a great financial strain (might be upwards of $20 per hour or $160 per day, if you work an eight-hour day). These are all things to consider if you want to work part-time and maximize your financial success while you raise your children.

Consulting

Consulting with other psychologists is an essential part of starting a new practice. Really think hard about this one. When finding a good person to consult with, please do not choose someone who is doing interesting work that is outside your scope. This may sound obvious, but you need to find someone who has a similar practice to yours.

Consulting with someone who has a similar practice is not exactly in the APA Code of Ethics, but it should be. Seriously, it is important to have someone in your areas of specialization that you can confide in and ask difficult clinical questions.

I looked into this when I was starting my practice. I had consulted with another psychologist who was doing quite different work than me, and we both felt that we were going different directions. It was not that we didn't understand each other or that it was a bad fit, personality-wise, but we were just mostly doing different work. I was doing mostly psych evals and he was doing 100 percent therapy. He did not do psych testing. I get random calls from people who see my sign outside, including a call from a psychologist down the street from me. We talked on the phone and agreed to meet.

Meeting Dr. Steve Johansson was a great experience. I knew right away that I would vibe well with him (this is the opportunity to use your clinical inference/judgment). We talked about both being former athletes, tall men in the field, etc., and we ended up talking about the therapy and psych evals that we were doing. Steve and I meet regularly for lunch. We vent to each other about the practice and talk about a few cases. We talk about ethical dilemmas or insanely interesting cases. We crack a few jokes about things that we have experienced. It is good to laugh with a colleague. We have similar humor, so I would also suggest choosing someone with a similar disposition. The laughing part can be big. I know that I feel a huge relief when laughing with Steve. Honestly, we don't have that many opportunities to laugh on a daily basis in our profession.

He has been in the field longer than I, so I typically ask more questions. But our practices are structured in a very similar manner. We have a lot in common, both personally and in our practices. We are a good fit for consulting. So when you choose someone to consult with, please consider these things. Find a good person, who is a good listener and will provide good feedback. Steve gives good feedback and is not afraid to tell me if I am doing something that he doesn't agree with. Find someone for whom you can provide feedback, too. I would strongly consider choosing someone who is in your age range, as well. Think about if your personality is a good match with them. If you are obsessive and extremely organized, do not find someone who is laid back or lackadaisical. Really do your research with this one. It is a great opportunity for professional growth. While this doesn't overtly give you money, it will help you financially down the line with the knowledge and growth that you gain in managing your practice. Seriously, you never know what kind of great tidbits of information that you can pick up from colleagues. Finally, I would strongly consider consulting at least one time per month. It is good to have consistency here.

I also do regular phone consultations with my friends and colleagues from San Diego who are now licensed. We talk about MMPI-2 personality profiles, Rorschachs, ethical dilemmas, anything really. These are people who are just a phone call away and if one person is busy I can always lean on someone else. It is really nice to have this option. I'm not saying that you have to, but it is a really nice safety net. Of course, it is essential to have a practice in strict accordance with the APA Code of Ethics, which states that if we have ethical dilemmas or major clinical questions that we should always consult. I also use this as a great chance to reconnect with my grad school friends. Really, consider doing this as well. Even if the colleagues are not in the same area as you, connect with someone on a regular basis.

Supervision

If you are starting a practice, you may need to get supervision, especially if you have many clinical questions. What makes a good supervisor? Like finding someone with whom you will consult well, consider finding someone with whom you relate well. If you are kind and empathic, find a kind and empathic supervisor. Use your clinical judgment here. Go ahead and call a few people. If you don't have a good feeling about the person, DON'T GO TO THEM! There are all types of psychologists who offer supervision and there are going to be many styles of supervising techniques. When you find the right person, you will know. It is best to see someone who can give you both positive and negative feedback, as you will make mistakes and it is good to have candid remarks about what you could have done better.

With psych testing, there can be some very difficult clinical questions, particularly if you are doing more complicated testing, such as evaluating individuals in a prison or a psychiatric hospital. There are going to be some very complex cases in these realms and it would be a good idea to consider getting supervision. If you feel that you are having a hard time managing stress or struggling with managing your practice, get supervision, before getting consultation. Major questions in clinical psychology require supervision rather than consultation. Paying for supervision is not fun, because it is usually very expensive. But it can be well worth it if you have to go to court on a case and you are asked, "Have you ever gotten clinical supervision after you have started your private practice?" Now I'm not saying that you need to do an hour of supervision a week. But seriously, think about going for 10 hours of supervision over a few months. Our profession can be complicated. Find someone who is an experienced, seasoned psychologist. They may also have some incredible advice to give in terms of ways to earn money. They might also give you referrals. You never know, there may be inherent financial assets of going to supervision as well.

Final Thoughts

Creating a financially successful practice in clinical psychology is not easy. It requires serious work and dedication that begins in undergrad and continues after grad school. I would argue that it requires a similar level of patience and diligence to finishing a doctoral program in clinical psychology. Now you have the tools to go forward in a profession that can change people's lives for the better, and give you a quality of life that is beyond the realm of possibility for many people. The American dream of hard work and justifiable rewards can be yours, as long as you remember that you will never attain the rewards without first mastering the hard work. My hope for you is that this book has given you a head start in the profession by showing you some of the pitfalls and the possibilities of a career in clinical psychology.

Index

Page numbers in *italics* indicate figures or tables.

Pickar, D. 125
plants, office 97
Popanz, Tim 153–4
positive outlook 103–4
postdoctoral hours 79–80, 90–1,
   111–12
practicum 63, 64, 72–4
prep courses: Examination for the
   Professional Practice of Psychology
   88–9; GRE 19, 20, 21
presentation, in communication 150–1
presentation anxiety 85–6
prison work 55–6
pro-bono work 153
procrastination 84
profession, ambivalence about 46
professional memberships 146–8,
   153, 164–5
professors 16, 64–6
psych assistants 135–7
psychiatric hospital internships
   69–70, 77
psychiatrists 44, 149
psychological associations, state
   146–8, 153, 164–5
psychological testing: compensation
   for 2, 70; graduate school 61–2,
   70–2; instruments 71, 127, 137,
   139; internships 71; supervision
   175–6
psychology classes, undergraduate 15,
   17–18
psychology major 26–7
psychotherapy *see* therapy
public service loan forgiveness 55

Ramsey, Dave 53–4
rate, lowering 114
reading 167
recommendation, letters of 16, 17, 22–3
record storage 98
referrals 156–8
reimbursement rates: children,
   working with 109; decline in

1–2, 7; insurance company 130;
   Master's-level clinicians 59;
   Medicare/Medicaid 116;
   work-injured patients 132–3, 135
relaxation training 166
reminder calls 120, 133
repayment options for student loans
   49–57
reports, Social Security 107–8
reputation 158–9
research for university professors 16
research grants 160
resilience 47–8
respect 148–9
restarting your practice 170, 172
rewards 13, 89
rugs, office 96, 97

sacrifices 43–6
salaries *see* compensation
saving 6–7, 49, 144, 145
school evaluations 110
Seattle area 75–6, 95–6
self-care 163–70
selling yourself 11
sickness 168–9
Siteskins.com 101–2
sleep 132, 165–6, 170
smoke, cigarette 118
socializing 147
Social Security evaluations 105–6,
   106–8
Spanish-language interpreters 134
staff, office 157
Stafford loans 48–9
state and government employees,
   working with 117–20
state and government work 105–9
state assistance evaluations 108–9
state evaluations, other 122–3
state exams 87
state psychological associations
   146–8, 153, 164–5
state taxes 100, 145

water 97, 166
websites 101–2
weekend escapes 163
weight-lifting 167
Winter, Deborah 17–18
witnesses, expert 125–8
work ethic 69–70, 78–9, 144–5,
 153–6

work-injured patients 98–9, 131–5
writing: APA style 16–17, 24, 68;
 on GRE 21–2; psych assistants,
 samples from 137

Yalom, Irvin D. 74
yield, bottom-line 46–7